INTELLIGENT
KNOWLEDGE BASED
SYSTEMS
an introduction

CW01067041

ASPECTS OF
INFORMATION TECHNOLOGY

This series is aimed primarily at final year undergraduate and postgraduate students of Electronics and Computer Science, and provides an introduction to research topics in Information Technology which are currently being translated into teaching course material. The series aims to build bridges between foundation material covered in the first two years of undergraduate courses and the major research topics now attracting interest within the field of IT.

The format of the series is deliberately different from that of typical research reference works within the fields of interest. Depth of coverage is restricted in favour of providing a readable and comprehensible introduction to each topic, and to keep costs within the requirements for a course textbook. Nevertheless, each book provides a comprehensive overview and introduction to its subject, aimed at conveying the key elements in an attractive and clear fashion.

Each chapter is terminated by a summary itemizing the key points contained within, and problems and exercises are provided where appropriate to enable the student to test his knowledge. For the serious student, each book contains a comprehensive further reading list of texts and key reference papers covering the field, as well as giving an indication of those journals which publish within the area.

Series editors: **A C Downton**   *University of Essex*
  R D Dowsing   *University of East Anglia*

INTELLIGENT KNOWLEDGE BASED SYSTEMS

an introduction

W. J. Black
Department of Computation, UMIST

 Van Nostrand Reinhold (UK) Co. Ltd

First published in 1986 by
Van Nostrand Reinhold (UK) Co. Ltd
Molly Millars Lane, Wokingham,
Berkshire, England

Typeset in 10/12pt Times by
Witwell, Ltd., Liverpool

Printed in Great Britain by
The Thetford Press Ltd,
Thetford, Norfolk

Library of Congress Cataloguing-in-Publication Data

Black, W. J.
  Intelligent knowledge based systems.

  Bibliography: p.
  Includes index.
  1. Artificial intelligence.   2. Expert systems
(Computer science)   I. Title.
Q335.B54   1986   006.3   86–18943
ISBN 0–442–31772–7

British Library Cataloguing in Publication Data

Black, W. J.
  Intelligent knowledge based systems.
  1. Expert systems (Computer science)
  I. Title
  006.3′ 3   QA76.76.E95

  ISBN 0–442–31772–7

CONTENTS

PREFACE

'Intelligent Knowledge Based Systems' will be abbreviated henceforward to 'IKBS'. The term refers to a range of computer applications that are more sophisticated than the clerical tasks forming the bulk of the work done by the majority of computers.

For about thirty years, Artificial Intelligence (AI) has been a recognized discipline within computer science. Researchers in AI have sought to build computer programs that undertake tasks that, if done by people, would be described as requiring intelligence. Following accepted scientific practice, it has been common to focus on simplified laboratory problems before attempting to solve real-world problems. Intellectual games like chess and go are quite successfully played by computers and the sort of problems posed in intelligence tests were tackled by the early problem solving programs. In the fields of vision and robotics, basic research has been done where the only objects to be identified are toy blocks in regular geometric shapes.

Around 1970 it was felt by some researchers that the basic concepts and methods of AI were sufficiently mature to be applied to selected real-world problems. At that time, the first expert systems, intelligent tutoring systems and natural language database query systems were constructed. The real-world problems could not be tackled by the very general and powerful methods that worked for the well-specified laboratory problems. A new approach was needed in which the specific knowledge of an application domain complemented the general purpose methods. In all these fields, there is plenty of fundamental research still to be done, but the relevance of AI to practical problems requiring intelligence has been demonstrated. This applied research has continued until in the late 1970s some systems left the laboratory to start earning their living in the commerical world.

Up to this point most of the work was carried out in the USA, but there has recently been an upsurge of interest elsewhere. The Japanese '5th Generation Computer' programme aims to provide intelligent systems on powerful but small and inexpensive personal computers by the end of the 1980s. The boldness of these plans has spurred on the governments in Europe and elsewhere to seek to coordinate national and international programmes of research and development to maintain competiveness in the IT industries. The term 'IKBS' has been generally preferred to 'AI' in these government initiatives partly because of the scepticism aroused by 'AI' and partly also to emphasize the applied nature of the work.

IKBS, then, can be regarded as applied AI. We can identify IKBS both by their external characteristics and their internal architecture. Externally, it must be tackling some problem worthy of the application of intelligence to its solution. In pure research AI, it is a difficult problem just defining 'intelligence', attracting the interest of philosophers as well as practitioners. In more pragmatic IKBS, we are concerned with providing systems that can lend assistance with technical and professional tasks. Examples of the tasks to which IKBS have been applied include medicine, engineering, geology, chemistry, education, architecture, librarianship and law. We will explore some of these IKBS applications more fully in the following chapters.

The major distinguishing feature of the internal architecture of IKBS is a partitioning into three main components: a knowledge base, a short-term working memory or 'database' and an inference mechanism (more affectedly an inference 'engine'). The inference mechanisms employed are general purpose and consist of theorem provers or search algorithms that have been developed in AI research. The knowledge base is domain specific. The IKBS architecture should enable new applications to be developed by changing only the knowledge base.

What is a knowledge base? The terminology clearly invites comparison with 'database'. A database is a pool of data structured to provide alternative access paths through related data to satisfy the needs of multiple operational data processing applications or *ad hoc* queries. A knowledge base is similar in the sense that it is a resource that can be accessed in different ways according to the requirements of a particular consultation or occasion of use. But 'knowledge' implies something more powerful than 'data'. The individual data items in a database represent the attributes of individual events and entities in the world, but they have no sense other than that given to them by the processing carried out on them by programs. 'Knowledge' implies an imposing of organizing principles on these isolated facts to provide an understanding of the world which is predictive and embraces or explains the individual facts. Knowledge is the product of learning. Wherever possible, a learner seeks to shake off the burden of memorizing large quantities of facts where some generalization or rule makes them redundant. A knowledge base, then, is an explicit structured representation of the underlying rules of some area of human expertise.

Some areas of expertise are clearly rule-based. As an ideal, legislative rules are quite definite about the conclusions that follow from their premises. However, in practice, there can be uncertainty about whether the premises apply in a given case. The rule-based nature of expertise is less clear in other professional areas. Medicine, for example, is underpinned by biological models of disease processes, but in clinical practice, uncertainty abounds. The existence and severity of symptoms is not always easy to assess. There are many cases where very different diseases present similar symptoms requiring 'differential diagnosis'. When a diagnosis is agreed on, there is uncertainty over treatments. Nevertheless, in writing down the knowledge of expert practitioners, a rule-based notation has been found to be useful.

In an expert system for such a domain, the inference mechanism needs to be able to reason under uncertainty. It is possible to apply *ad hoc* scoring procedures which can be applied in particular programs but the IKBS approach is to consider uncertainty as a more pervasive phenomenon and to treat it systematically.

THE PLAN OF THIS BOOK

Chapter 1 introduces the idea of expert systems and focuses on examples and then on the characteristics of such systems.

This is followed by an appreciation of Prolog, a programming language based on the idea that programming can be viewed as deduction over a knowledge base structured in a logical formalism. Our appreciation of Prolog concludes with an illustrative expert system 'Shell' written in the language.

Chapter 3 introduces the topic of knowledge representation which is fundamental to all applications of IKBS. We describe several alternative forms of representation, some of which have been used in expert systems and some in other knowledge-based applications.

Chapter 4 examines the process of developing an expert system, looking at the steps in the 'life cycle' of an expert system and some of the alternative approaches to implementation.

Chapter 5 considers two different aspects of the relationship of knowledge-based systems to processes of learning. First we consider the problem of how a knowledge based system can acquire new knowledge for itself, since the time and cost of developing knowledge bases is a major inhibiting factor in the spread of these applications. The second aspect is the contribution a knowledge based system can make to human learning. Here we consider the similarities and differences between expert systems on the one hand and intelligent computer aided instruction systems on the other. The former are concerned with bringing knowledge to bear on the solution of a problem whereas the latter are concerned with the transfer of the knowledge to the student.

Next we consider natural language and the computer. It is already possible to interact with commercial information systems in apparently natural language, and other interactive computer applications including expert systems and ICAI have a need for natural user interfaces. Chapter 6 introduces some of the basic principles of language description and processing and looks in detail at an approach based directly on Prolog.

Chapter 7 considers the place of semantics in language understanding and describes an approach to natural language understanding which emphasizes its knowledge based nature.

Chapter 8 follows with a discussion of a number of intelligent user interfaces or 'front ends' to database and operating systems as well as to expert systems.

READERSHIP

The book is intended to support an introductory course in IKBS, which usually has the status of an option in the second or final year of a degree course or in a conversion course in computer science, computer studies or information technology. No specific prerequisite courses are assumed, and the book may also be of interest to students of related disciplines in which IKBS may be applied. It may also serve as a readable introduction to the field for computing professionals. The informal treatment should make it reasonably accessible to the interested layman.

ACKNOWLEDGEMENTS

I am grateful to my colleague, Gerard Conroy, for reading drafts of most of the book and pointing out some of the places where the text was less clear than it ought to have been. I have also benefited from feedback from students on the MSc conversion course in Computation on some of the material.

1

EXPERT SYSTEMS

This chapter introduces the idea of an expert system as the most typical application of knowledge based systems. Rather than offer a precise definition, we approach the task by first looking at some examples of expert systems and then contrasting a number of related types of interactive system that use different methods. Finally, the main architectural and operational features of expert systems are outlined.

In the Preface, we introduced the idea of a knowledge based system as a computer system that embodies an explicit representation of knowledge of an application domain. The knowledge base has to be a separate component of the system, the other parts of which are domain independent. Expert systems are a subset of knowledge based systems, but one that is not easy to define.

For some practitioners in the field the defining characteristic is the level of competence of the system. A system can be said to be an expert system if it performs at or near the level of human experts. For others it's the area of application: an expert system is one that is applied to the difficult and important problems that we associate with calling in human experts as consultants.

Another important feature of expert systems is their mode of operation. If we consult a human expert for advice, we expect to be given a justification of the reasoning that led to the expert conclusion, and an expert system should operate in the same way too.

1.1 EXAMPLES OF EXPERT SYSTEMS

Attempts of defining a general concept in this way can be futile in the absence of knowledge of particular examples. We will examine the capabilities of the more prominent expert systems in the research literature before focussing on how such systems are constructed and used.

1.1.1 MYCIN

The best known example of an expert system is MYCIN. MYCIN was developed largely by Dr Edward Shortliffe, a member of the Heuristic Programming Project in Stanford University, in the early 1970s. Its task is to act as a consultant on both diagnosis and treatment of infectious diseases. Before using the program, a doctor will have laboratory reports on cultures taken from the patient. The organisms found therein should be described but not necessarily identified.

The MYCIN dialogue starts with a request for the basic patient data (name, age and sex). The doctor is then asked about infections at individual sites in the body, then cultures taken from those sites, and ultimately about the shape and other observable characteristics of the individual organisms found in those cultures. Other pertinent facts include the dates and times at which the cultures were taken.

A particular feature of MYCIN is that it deals with unreliable or uncertain knowledge. A particular set of observations may provide only suggestive evidence for a diagnosis, not a definite conclusion. The certainty of a conclusion has to be recorded, and may be augmented if there is further confirming evidence, or decreased if there is opposing evidence. The certainty may be expressed as a decimal fraction on a scale between 1 for certain, through 0 for 'don't know', to –1 for 'certainly not'. Users of the system may also express their lack of confidence in observations, but this is not encouraged in MYCIN, since most questions are put directly.

Because of the uncertainty of the underlying medical knowledge, the system reports its analysis and advice also on the certainty scale. MYCIN offers conclusions about the identity of the infecting organisms and also about the recommended treatment. The treatment typically includes drugs which will deal with the organisms identified and also with other organisms whose presence is inferred but not known for certain.

1.1.2 PROSPECTOR

Another of the well-known systems from the research literature is PROSPECTOR. As its name would suggest, this system's expertise lies in exploration geology. Drilling test bores to confirm the presence of valuable mineral deposits is expensive, so experts are relied on to select reasonable prospects before further exploration is done. As in medical diagnosis, the system seeks to establish a level of confidence in a range of possible conclusions from empirical evidence supplied by a less expert practitioner.

Uncertain evidence offered by the user is more of a feature in PROSPECTOR than in MYCIN. The user of the system has to be a geologist, since the observable evidence that PROSPECTOR needs includes the visible landforms, the exposed rocks and their appearance and texture.

1.1.3 XCON (R1)

XCON started out with the obscure name 'R1'. This was a play on the old saying, 'For years I've wanted to become a (knowledge) engineer. Now at last I R1 (are one).' This name has nothing to do with the application, which is the configuration of VAX computers. Minicomputers like the VAX are not delivered as an off-the-shelf package, but are typically sold with a specific configuration of input, output and storage devices, processor power, main memory and software for a particular customer. There are interdependencies between these options, for example where additional devices require additional memory. Each configurable device also requires additional hardware components, and these have to be laid out on circuit boards, and the circuit boards connected to backplanes inside cabinets. An individual customer's configuration may be unique, but for DEC to satisfy the order competitively, the design must be cost-effective, avoiding unneccessary components and cabinets.

In five years XCON has processed nearly 100000 customer orders, each in a relatively small amount of computer time. It does not operate as an interactive dialogue as many expert systems do, but starts out with full data on the customer's requirements. (This is now provided through another expert program XSEL – expert selling consultant.) The form of the expert knowledge is rules as in other systems, but they are processed in a data-driven strategy.

R1 was developed as a prototype using a pre-existing rule-based system generator known as OPS4. The prototype was built in about three man-months, and it was gradually refined against many test cases, reaching a usable state in about a year. It has been accepted that mistakes will be made, and the program, as XCON, now embodies over 4000 rules and has been through a rational reconstruction with new software as well as steady enhancement. This development history is typical of expert systems, and will be discussed further in Chapter 4. What is significant about XCON is not any intrinsically unique features, but that it is one of the first systems to pay its way in the commercial world.

As these examples show, expert systems may be characterized functionally, i.e. by task. This is generally to apply professional expertise within a specialized domain. They may also be recognized by the manner of their use, usually an interactive dialogue where the user supplies the parameters of an individual problem case. However there are many other classes of interactive system which are not generally described as expert systems. Some of them even tackle the same or similar problems. Before discussing the operational features of expert systems, we will consider a number of instances of systems whose approach contrasts with that of expert systems.

1.2   WHAT AN EXPERT SYSTEM IS NOT

A number of related types of computer application are discussed below for contrast.

1.2.1   Medical diagnosis by statistical means

Rule-based expert systems normally contain rules that are derived from the subjective judgement of a human expert rather than from objective empirical observation. However, medical practitioners are well accustomed to statistical methods in the basic scientific work in their discipline. Indeed this disposition sometimes brings them into conflict with members of the public who apply other forms of reasoning in such areas as vaccination policy and hospital obstetric practices. The potential users of a computer diagnostic aid, junior hospital doctors, are likely, because of their medical education, to be more impressed by a statistical justification of diagnostic conclusions than one based on the sequencing and selection of questions concerning the patient's signs, symptoms and history.

To develop a diagnostic system based on statistics, the knowledge-base of judgemental rules is supplanted by a contingency table: On one dimension of this matrix are the hypothesized diseases, and on the other are the clinical observables. The matrix elements are the frequencies with which each hypothesis–evidence pair occurred within an overall survey sample. This statistical database is deployed in individual cases by direct application of Bayes' rule (which is used also in expert systems for handling uncertainty, see below), to give a probability for each of the diseases under consideration. This is computationally more trivial than the expert system approach, and with a suitably coded data capture form, input can be very quick and may be delegated by the doctor to a clerical assistant. Work of this nature has been carried on for many years now, for example by de Dombal (discussed briefly in Hayes-Roth *et al.* 1983, pp. 250–1).

One of the prerequisites for this work is that a statistical database is to hand. With certain classes of illness, inevitably leading to surgical intervention or death if not treated (e.g. ulcers, cancers and certain heart complaints), it is possible ultimately to be quite certain about the disease that was responsible for a given symptom set. However, for a range of conditions, including infectious diseases, often successfully treated non-surgically (and where treatment is the same for different diseases), such definite conclusions may never be possible. In many areas of medical expertise, then, adequate statistical data are not available, and Bayesian databases cannot be built. Furthermore definitions of diseases and symptoms may vary between individual doctors and over time. Often definitions are merely operational in that they refer to a syndrome or set of symptoms whose cause is not understood.

It is also the case that expert systems in medicine are not confined to the diagnosis task. MYCIN, PUFF and the Digitalis Advisor are all concerned with the treatment or management of a known condition, rather than (or as well as) the diagnosis of the condition.

1.2.2 Browsing and prompting systems

The next example of a contrast to the expert systems approach comes also from the medical domain, but as in the last example, the principles concerned have wider application. The approach taken in one project for computer-aided diagnosis, the RECONSIDER system (Tuttle *et al.*, 1983), has been to apply simple information retrieval techniques. Instead of a knowledge base comprising expert-derived rules of the type employed in MYCIN and discussed below, this system employed a list of standard names of diseases with their associated symptoms and body systems, and a thesaurus of synonyms as its only sources of medical knowledge. The machine-readable 'Current Medical Information and Terminology' stored the names and attributes of 3262 different diseases. From this, an inverted index was constructed which stored information about each term's position in the original entry.

In a dialogue with the system, the user would indicate the attribute context (for example signs and symptoms, or 'all') and some terms (for example, 'abdominal pain'). The system found pointers to the disease entries where the words occurred in the same clause and attribute context and reported a 'selectivity score' indicating what proportion of all diseases were indexed by the given terms. The user could either supply additional terms to get a more selective score, or review a ranked list of diseases making use of information displayed to suggest further terms, or to come to his/her own conclusions about the diagnosis. The goal of the system is not to do the diagnosis for the doctor, but to provide a useful prompt to ensure nothing is overlooked. The system could be said to achieve this goal if the correct diagnosis in tests occurred near the top of the ranked list. RECONSIDER's performance was contrasted with published results with two expert systems and was considered to be at least as good in terms of diagnostic accuracy although direct comparison was not possible.

An important question prompted by this system is: 'What is the correct partnership between the computer and the user in a system to be used in expert problem solving?' Should the computer be used to take on the decision-making task itself, leaving the user as a spectator, or should we prefer to cast it as a humble provider of information to support human decision making? Research workers in all disciplines have at their disposal vast databases of scientific literature from which to select items relevant to a particular problem. Here the computer retrieval software acts as a mere indexing and filing system, leaving the researcher the intellectual task of extracting the knowledge from the author's text.

1.2.3   Computer-aided instruction systems

The contrast between this application and expert systems is that the latter are concerned with solving a current problem, whereas the former aims to develop the ability of the user to solve problems in the future. The aims sound very different, but the methods may turn out less so in practice. In all forms of education and training, it is recognized that people do not learn by being told (especially being told once only), but need to be given practice in applying general principles to many individual problems. If computer systems are to be used in support of the learning of general principles, then the use of those principles when applied to specific problems needs to be made explicit. For example, Clancey (1983) found that MYCIN was not entirely suitable for clinical education, because it did not incorporate the same reasoning strategies as clinical experts, and because it did not connect the judgemental rules used in diagnosis with the general principles taught in medical school.

If the requirement is for low-level training rather than education for problem-solving, then software tools associated with computer-aided instruction may be more appropriate than those for developing expert systems. Having said that, one of the spin-offs from development of expert systems is that techniques are percolating down to the provision of aids for less expert work, and some expert system shells, designed for 'text animation' are particularly suitable for developing such dialogues.

Considerable work has been done in the IKBS community on the direct application of intelligent techniques in education. This work is generally described under the banner of Intelligent Computer Aided Instruction (ICAI), and will be examined more closely in Chapter 5.

1.2.4   Help systems

Many interactive computer systems require a large amount of input from the user. If the system is in habitual use, users will typically prefer a relatively terse form of input prompting, whereas for new users much description is needed to explain the meaning of the data values to be input. One way of satisfying both classes of user is to provide a contextual help facility: A help key is provided with which the user can interrupt the normal flow of the dialogue to obtain a display of text, explaining the meaning of the data item currently being solicited more fully than its standard prompt. Forms packages produced by most mini- and mainframe computer manufacturers or as part of 'fourth-generation languages' (4GLs) provide the means of generating contextual help in data-capture programs.

If the procedures to be followed in a putative expert system are reasonably easy to describe algorithmically and the application is not of a professional-level expertise, then a 4GL approach is indicated. This will probably be the case with a great many proposals for expert systems which arise within DP departments and other computer users. The superficial resemblance to an expert system arises because of the explanatory help requirement. It is emphasized that the explanation of individual data items and the justification of conclusions and the line of reasoning that established them are not the same.

1.2.5 Planning systems

Planning systems are a contrast with the foregoing and to expert systems. Planning is another area of AI application but operates at the opposite end of a scale on which the amount of domain knowledge is measured. Whereas an expert system embodies a large amount of domain knowledge, a planning system uses a more sparse deductive model. A planner for a specific domain uses a list of operations completely defined in terms of their effect on the working database which models the current state of the object 'world'. The initial state of the world can be considered as a set of axioms and the desired state as a theorem to be proved. The deductive component of the system attempts to prove that a set of applications of the basic operations results in the final state. We discuss planning in Chapter 5.

1.3 INTERNAL STRUCTURE OF EXPERT SYSTEMS

It is also important to consider the internal or structural and operational features of expert systems. Details vary from one system to another according to both the demands of the application and the approach taken by the developer, but the following features are common to many expert systems:

- Explicit representation of domain knowledge.
- A general-purpose inference mechanism providing control.
- Provision for reasoning with uncertain evidence and knowledge.
- Provision of justification, explanation and other run-time user support.

We consider each in turn.

1.4 EXPLICIT REPRESENTATION OF DOMAIN KNOWLEDGE

Within the fields of AI and IKBS generally, a number of different notations and formalisms have been employed to represent knowledge. All have been used singly or in combination in expert systems, but by far the most popular is the **production rule** notation. We review the alternative formalisms in Chapter 3, but for the present we will illustrate the representation of expert knowledge using production rules exclusively.

1.4.1 Production rule representation of knowledge

Figure 1.1 shows an example rule in MYCIN style, translated into a readable form.

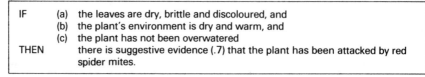

```
IF      (a)  the leaves are dry, brittle and discoloured, and
        (b)  the plant's environment is dry and warm, and
        (c)  the plant has not been overwatered
THEN         there is suggestive evidence (.7) that the plant has been attacked by red
             spider mites.
```

Fig. 1.1 Example production rule.

Each rule has two essential parts, the **premises** or **antecedents** and the **action** (or **conclusion** or **consequents**). The premise may be a single condition, or as in Fig. 1.1, it may be a conjunction. In principle it may be an arbitrary Boolean expression, but many expert systems are a little more constrained, as an aid to both clarity and implementation. Conclusions may also be compounded: In some MYCIN rules for example, alternative conclusions follow from the same premises, each with its own certainty factor.

The separation of knowledge and control permits the run-time facilities of providing on-demand explanation and justification. The simplicity of the rule format provides a good communication medium between the system and the user and also between the system developer and expert informant.

A typical expert system has a knowledge base comprising many such rules. The individual rules appear trivial, but the power of the system lies in the aggregate of all the rules. To get a clearer idea of the significance of the use of production rules, it is helpful to contrast the idea of a **production system** with that of an **algorithm**.

An individual production rule appears familiar to a programmer or systems analyst, who will note a resemblance to the selection construction used in programming languages, 'Structured English' or decision tables and trees.

Despite the overall resemblance, there are several important points of distinction:

1   There is nothing in production rules corresponding to the **sequence** and **iteration** constructs of programs and their underlying

algorithms. These constructs are concerned with the control of a program. In a production system, all matters of control are delegated to a general inference mechanism whose characteristics we examine below. It is an important feature of the IKBS approach that domain knowledge can be entirely expressed in a **declarative** manner and does not need to be embedded within explicit instructions for how it is to be applied.

2 Production rules do not use complex nested IFs, nor do they specify what happens if conditions are not met. Naturally this simplification of the rule format makes life easier for the inference engine builder, but it is also beneficial in its clarity. Nested IF constructions are notoriously difficult to understand and they and ELSE constructs used in algorithms require careful attention to be given to the range or scope of the various conditions. This is recognized by injunctions in programming textbooks to incorporate contrary conditions as comments.

3 The principle of **single assignment** should ideally be followed in the action or conclusion part of the rules. By this we mean that a proposition or variable is assigned a value only once. If a value is known, then that value is used whenever the item is accessed. The value is never replaced by another assignment. Figure 1.2 illustrates a set of rules which violates the single assignment principle.

rule 1	IF insurance group is 1 THEN premium is 200
rule 2	IF driver is over 30 THEN premium = premium −50
rule 3	IF excess payment accepted THEN premium = premium ×0.9
rule 4	IF no claims protection accepted THEN premium = premium +5

Fig. 1.2 Rules employing multiple assignment.

We can immediately see a problem with rules stated in this way. The sequence in which the rules are applied is critical to the result. In a production system, the inference engine 'decides' when to apply each rule, so rules like these cannot be used. We can avoid multiple assignment by using additional data items such as 'age allowance', 'excess factor' and a single assignment to premium. The principle at work here, as in applicative programming, is to avoid side-effects.

This principle has not been followed in the rule-base of the MYCIN system and leads to an anomaly we will consider when we consider MYCIN's treatment of uncertain knowledge below. Where MYCIN departs from single assignment, it is to permit **self-referencing** rules. A self-referencing rule is used in such circumstances as where a rule applies only if there is already some confirming evidence for its conclusion. This situation could be handled by other means, and indeed PROSPECTOR recognizes 'contextual relations' between propositions for just this kind of circumstance.

4 **Rule-independence** results from the separation of rules from control and the single-assignment principle. Any rule can be meaningfully read independently of any other. It is possible to **change** a rule without worrying about side-effects (although of course it is not always possible to delete a rule if its conclusion is required in the premise of another rule).

1.5 THE INFERENCE ENGINE IN AN EXPERT SYSTEM

Expert systems may contain from about 50 to several thousand rules. In a consultation the task is to apply all those that are relevant to the problem at hand (and avoid those that are not).

We made the point in discussing production rules that the knowledge-base contains no information about how to find the rules that apply and when to evaluate them. In contrast to a conventional program, the production system approach is to use a general-purpose control structure or inference mechanism.

An individual rule is said to 'fire' when it is selected for evaluation. Once its premises (or antecedents) have all been evaluated, the truth of its conclusions (or consequents) can be determined.

A mechanism is needed for selecting which rules to fire and in what order. Two alternative strategies can be identified: **forward chaining** and **backward chaining**. In either case, 'chaining' refers to a chain of inferences or line of reasoning. Forward chaining is a line of reasoning that starts from known facts and fires rules to infer conclusions. A backward chain of inferences starts with a conclusion that we want to prove and then fires rules which can establish that conclusion. Where the conditions in a rule are unknown, they can be established by either recursively firing other rules or by direct questioning of the user. Forward and backward chaining are sometimes referred to as 'data-driven' and 'goal-directed' inference respectively.

An illustration of forward chaining

For a simple example of forward chaining we turn to a familiar puzzle studied as an example of human problem solving by the psychologist Allen Newell. In cryptarithmetic puzzles, we are given an arithmetic problem and its solution with the digits coded as letters. The task is to break the code using the rules of arithmetic and find the digit represented by each letter. For example, in

```
    D  O  N  A  L  D
 +  G  E  R  A  L  D
 =  R  O  B  E  R  T      given D = 5
```

we can start from the known fact, $D = 5$. From that, we can infer that $T = 0$ and that 1 is carried to column 2. Having made those inferences, we can then make further ones: $R = (2*L) \text{ MOD } 10 + 1$, and from that, R is odd, then R is a member of the set $\{1, 3, 7, 9\}$ (since $R <> 5$). We can continue with this reasoning until we have a consistent set of values for each letter.

A forward-chaining inference engine operates in a cycle. In each cycle it examines the current state of its database and fires those rules whose antecedents are satisfied, putting the new conclusions in the database. The cycles stop when no more rules can fire.

An illustration of backward chaining

Planning a railway journey is a good example of backward chaining. To know when to leave home for the station, we have to take account of our final goal of arriving at the destination in time for an appointment. First we consider how to get from the nearest railway station to the destination and how long it will take. Next, we look up the railway timetable for the line to that station and find the nearest arrival time before the desired arrival time. We then work backwards to the departure time from the first station on that line which is on our intended route. From there we refer to the timetable for the route which gets us to that station from somewhere nearer home, and so on until we find the departure time from our local station.

A clear advantage of the backward chaining approach is that it is goal-directed, that is, the search for the next step to apply is highly constrained. In planning the railway journey, we would make many pointless references between timetables if we choose starting times at random.

1.5.1 Choice of inference strategy

When do we use a forward-chaining strategy and when do we use backward chaining? The answer depends on features of the application. More systems use backward chaining, since it is much easier to focus the search strategy in a backward chaining system. The mechanism is relatively straightforward and the questions asked of the user are more naturally grouped together around the current goal. It is easy to justify the line of reasoning under this strategy, as we shall see shortly.

It has also been argued that backward chaining more closely follows the course of human problem solving. Starting with a hypothesis and attempting to either confirm or refute it is the standard method of experimental science. A 'top-down' approach where we start from a broad statement of high-level goals is the accepted wisdom in computing, too.

However, human problem solving does not always follow this pattern as our example above showed. In the cryptarithmetic puzzle, the top-level goal is to find the digit corresponding to each letter. If we took the solution of the code for an arbitrary letter as our first subgoal, we might well establish a very long inference chain before succeeding. It is clear that immediate progress can be made with the given fact that D corresponds to 5.

In expert problem solving too there is a place for forward chaining. It can be argued that systems like MYCIN only work at all in circumstances where the user has a good idea what the possible conclusions are. Backward chaining fits in well with the idea of consulting an expert for a 'differential diagnosis' or a second opinion, but it does not model the reasoning process of the general practitioner who had to establish some hypotheses from the clinical evidence in the first place. Extending the expert-systems concept from professional to lay use may well result in more emphasis being given to forward chaining.

Of the well-known expert systems, MYCIN and PROSPECTOR use backward chaining, but XCON (R1) uses forward chaining. In the latter case, interaction with the user is not so significant. An **embedded** expert system which forms part of a real-time monitoring and control system may well be employed to react appropriately to exceptional input events, and forward chaining would be the natural way to implement this.

In some applications, it will be desirable to adopt a control mechanism which chains forward and backwards, and indeed systems have been constructed which do this. It is also desirable, where the expert's problem-solving strategy differs greatly from any of the mechanical inference strategies, that the former should be adopted by the machine. This implies a more sophisticated system where in addition to the domain knowledge in the knowledge base, there is a body of 'meta-rules' concerning the strategy experts actually use. Kidd (1985) found that expert electronics fault-finders used a strategy of always eliminating faults that were easy to detect first. Only when these tests failed would the more troublesome or expensive tests be made.

1.6 REASONING WITH UNCERTAIN EVIDENCE AND KNOWLEDGE

Not all expert systems deal with uncertainty. However, it is one feature which enables new classes of problem to be tackled by computer, since most applications hitherto have assumed that the computer is capable of only strict logical deduction. Uncertainty can arise in two contexts within an expert system.

1   The user can be uncertain of the answer to a question. For example the rule in Fig. 1.1 incorporated the condition 'the plant has not been overwatered'. A user of an expert program incorporating this rule may not know how the plant has been treated in the past. An appropriate answer might be 'don't know' or if there is some circumstantial evidence from the soil, then 'probably'. Often this kind of uncertainty is confused in systems with variables that have a value which can be supplied subjectively. For example,

'How overweight is the patient?'

is not the same as

'How certain are you that the patient is overweight?'

2   The rule may not establish a conclusion with certainty. In the geological context, it is likely that a favourable surface environment can never prove conclusively the existence of a deposit below ground, but only to a degree of certainty. It may be that further rules can add or detract from this certainty. In this case the expert knowledge is uncertain, and it doesn't matter how certain the user is of his evidence.

As a consequence, the system may be uncertain of its conclusions. This can arise where either uncertain evidence has been supplied or rules have been fired which lead to uncertain conclusions. It may be that a number of competing conclusions are presented together, each with a different degree of certainty.

To accommodate uncertainty, an expert system must have some way of calculating its confidence in a conclusion in proportion to the weight of the evidence. A number of different methods have been used in different expert systems, some based on probability and some on a more subjective notion of the characteristics of commonsense reasoning. We examine three different ways of handling uncertainty – a simple fuzzy logic, a statistical approach based on Bayes' rule, and the certainty calculus used in MYCIN.

1.6.1 Fuzzy logic

A simple method for combining the certainty of the conditions that are either conjoined or disjoined in the premise of a rule has been labelled 'fuzzy logic'. It has been employed in several systems including both MYCIN and PROSPECTOR, alongside more complex ways of handling uncertainty. Under this scheme, the three-conditions rule in Fig. 1.1 being conjoined (ANDed), the conclusion would be assigned the *minimum* of the certainties of its antecedents. This seems a natural extension of our interpretation of the Boolean logic of 'AND'. Correspondingly, if we have a rule in which the conditions are disjoined or ORed, the conclusion is given the maximum certainty of its antecedents. The fuzzy logic interpretation of NOT is the complement of the antecedent.

A major limitation of the fuzzy logic scheme outlined above is that it treats all the conjuncts as of equal weight in principle, but in practice the value of the conclusion depends solely on whichever condition receives the minimum certainty (or maximum if the conditions are disjoined): The denial of a single condition within a conjunction will result in the denial of the conclusion, no matter how positive the user is about the other conditions. Often also some conditions are more significant than others, and should affect the outcome of the rule proportionately. Both of these problems are tackled by the Bayesian and MYCIN approaches to uncertainty, although more sensitive fuzzy logic definitions for the operators can be devised.

There is more to fuzzy logic than we have indicated so far. An important feature is the way linguistic expressions, such as 'not very' are mapped on to fuzzy truth values, although this is the subject of controversy amongst logicians, cf. Haack (1980).

1.6.2 Bayesian inference

Certainty is subjective. Users in answering questions and experts in estimating the likelihood of a conclusion are both providing not a probability but a degree of belief. To deal with uncertainty at all in a computer system, it is necessary to give each proposition a numeric weight corresponding to the degree of belief. A **certainty calculus** is needed which will use the combination of certainties of the conditions to establish that of the conclusion. The calculus needs to have certain basic mathematical properties, principally that the certainty of the conclusion must be on the same scale as that used to express the certainty of the conditions and that the operations are well defined and consistent over the whole range of values. One way to guarantee that the calculus has these properties is to 'import' one which is known to have them. Statistical probability theory is the obvious candidate. This can be applied in the context of a production system having rules of the form:

if E then H

where E represents an observable piece of evidence and H the hypothesis to be tested.

In processing this rule in an inference engine, the task is to update the probability of H using

a   its prior probability, i.e. the probability of H independent of any associated evidence for or against H, and
b   the truth or otherwise of E.

Bayes' rule gives a formulation for this:

$$P(H|E) = \frac{P(E|H).P(H)}{P(E)}$$

To make the formula readable, '|' should be rendered as 'given'. Thus $P(H|E)$ means the probability that H is true given E is known to be true, whereas $P(H)$ is the probability of H being true without taking E into account. $P(H)$ denotes the **prior** probability of H.

This is not the place for a formal derivation of Bayes' rule, but an illustration of it is given in Fig. 1.3, in the form of a Venn diagram.

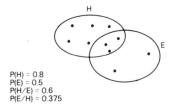

P(H) = 0.8
P(E) = 0.5
P(H/E) = 0.6
P(E/H) = 0.375

Fig. 1.3 Illustration of Bayes' rule.

The dots in the diagram represent the individual possible states of affairs in a universe of discourse. The dots enclosed by the ring labelled 'H' are those in which the hypothesis H holds true. The evidence E holds true in those enclosed by the ring labelled 'E'.

In statistical theory, there is no difference in kind between an hypothesis and an instance of evidence for it. Both are observable events, and their prior and conditional probabilities should have been established empirically before Bayes' rule can properly be applied.

If we use the rule for subjective certainties instead of probabilities, there is a difficulty in obtaining reasonable estimates of $P(H)$, $P(E)$ and $P(E|H)$ from an expert informant. Fortunately, the rule can be reformulated algebraically in terms of ratios which have more subjective meaning. Firstly, the probability of an event H can be expressed as **odds** using the relationship

$$O(H) = \frac{P(H)}{1 - P(H)}$$

Secondly, a **likelihood ratio** (LS, standing for 'logical sufficiency') can be defined:

$$LS = \frac{P(E|H)}{P(E|\tilde{H})}$$

LS is a factor saying how much more likely it is that a given evidence should be associated with the truth of an hypothesis than with its denial. This ratio can be used to establish posterior odds as follows:

$$O(H|E) = LS.O(H)$$

The expert informant is asked to provide a value for LS which is a much more intuitive concept than probability. LS is positive and greater than unity. Another ratio LN ('logical necessity'), allows the odds on an hypothesis to be updated given the absence of the evidence:

$$O(H|\tilde{}E) = LN.O(H)$$

where LN lies between 0 and 1. Again this factor can be supplied by the expert informant.

The LS and LN ratios are attached separately to each of the antecedents of a rule, and a prior probability of the conclusion also needs to be declared. A notation such as that shown in Fig. 1.4 can express all of this information.

The plant has been attacked by red spider mites (PRIOR 0.05)
IF
    The leaves are dry, brittle and discoloured (LS 20, LN 0.1).
    The plant's environment is dry and warm (LS 7, LN 0.2).
    The plant has not been overwatered (LS 5, LN 0.5).

Fig. 1.4 Sample Bayesian rule.

The rule is able to state that the first condition, the evidence of the condition of the leaves, is much more crucial to the probability of the conclusion than are the other two conditions. Worked examples of how the certainties of the conditions variously contribute to that of the conclusion illustrate this:

1   The user is certain of the first condition, doesn't know about the second, and is certain that the third is false. The inference machine will first convert the prior probability to odds (0.05/(1–0.05) = 0.053). The prior odds will then be multiplied by 20 (LS for condition 1), 1 (since condition 2 not known) and 0.5 (LN for condition 3), giving posterior odds of 0.53, and a posterior probability of 0.53/(1+0.53) = 0.346.

2   In this case the user is certain that the first condition is false, unsure of the second, and certain the last is true. This time the posterior odds are multiplied by 0.1, 1 and 5 to give 0.0265 (probability 0.0258).

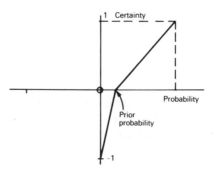

Fig. 1.5 Relationship between certainty and probability.

In both cases certainties can be mapped on to probabilities. On a scale of 5 (certain) through 0 (unknown) to –5 (denial is certain), 5 maps to a probability of 1, 0 to the prior probability and –5 to 0. Intermediate values are interpolated linearly as shown in Fig. 1.5.

Systems may use logarithmic scales to aid efficiency by avoiding multiplications and divisions, and may use variants of the notation suggested above, but the essential feature of the Bayesian approach is that it is possible to weight the contribution made by different evidence factors to the certainty of a conclusion.

1.6.3 The MYCIN approach to uncertainty

In MYCIN and its derivatives, a certainty scale of 1 to –1 has been employed. To see how evidence can be combined, we will use the example MYCIN-like rule shown earlier in Fig. 1.1 as context:

IF   (a) the leaves are dry, brittle and discoloured, and
        (b) the plant's environment is dry and warm, and
        (c) the plant has not been overwatered
THEN   there is suggestive evidence (.7) that the plant has been attacked by red spider mites.

Using this rule alone, the highest possible certainty for a spider mite attack is 0.7. This will occur only if all of the antecedents are known with certainty. A lesser certainty of the conclusion can be computed by the product of the fuzzy logic AND of the antecedents and 0.7. It is possible to be more certain of the conclusion if another rule leads to the same conclusion. If for example, there is a rule which concludes:

THEN   there is suggestive evidence (.5) that the plant has been attacked by red spider mites.

how do we compute the certainty of the conclusion using 0.7 and 0.5? The formulae used in MYCIN are:

$$\text{Cnew (C1, C2)} = \text{C1} + \text{C2} \times (1 - \text{C1}) \qquad \{\text{C1, C2 both} > 0\}$$
$$\text{Cnew (C1, C2)} = -\text{Cnew} (-\text{C1}, -\text{C2}) \qquad \{\text{C1, C2 both} < 0\}$$
$$\text{Cnew (C1, C2)} = \frac{\text{C1} + \text{C2}}{-\min(|\text{C1}|, |\text{C2}|)} \qquad \{\text{C1} \times \text{C2} < 0\}$$

These formulae guarantee that the combined certainty takes account of both values and still lies within the certainty range. In this instance, the combined certainty is 0.85.

1.6.4 Drawbacks with the MYCIN approach to uncertainty

When a conclusion cannot be established with a certainty greater than 0.2, it is treated as false. This results in a magnification of the negative effect such a conclusion can have upon further conclusions for which it is a premise. There is also a degree of arbitrariness in the treatment of conclusions established with certainty. If one value for an attribute is certain (+1.0), then all other values for that attribute are deleted from the dynamic database (including those that have previously been established as certain).

Another problem arises because rules are allowed to be self-referencing. This may be quite legitimate, as in the case where a conclusion is regarded as possible, but further evidence is required to be more certain. If it is not regarded as possible, then the user is not to be troubled with irrelevant questions regarding this other evidence. This situation can be encoded in two (or more) rules where one concludes with a low certainty, and another self-referencing rule has the proposition as both a premise and a conclusion. If there are two or more self-referencing rules leading to the same conclusion, the order in which they are fired can make a difference to the certainty of the conclusion.

All of these difficulties with MYCIN's handling of uncertainty are discussed more fully in Cendrowska and Bramer (1984).

1.7 JUSTIFICATION AND EXPLANATION

As we saw earlier in this chapter, other approaches compete with expert systems in such areas as medical diagnosis. Against this background, one of the claimed advantages for expert systems is that they do not simply conclude with the pronouncement of a diagnosis, but are also able to justify it. The user of a diagnostic program will have more confidence in it if this is provided. Alternatively, he is more likely to be able to see where it has gone wrong if the knowledge base is defective. In addition, users may require explanation or amplification of the meaning of a question the system asks of them.

Explanation or amplification is generally provided in most expert systems by simply having help text associated with each question the system may ask of the user. In this respect, an expert system is no different from any interactive program following current good practice.

In a backward-chaining production system, rudimentary justification facilities can be provided mechanically without any additions to the knowledge base. We will examine how this is done below, then consider the shortcomings of the approach and some of the alternatives that have been put forward in the recent research literature.

1.7.1 'Why' justification

In a system including the rule given in Fig. 1.1 within its knowledge base, part of the conversation with the user might go like this:

```
How certain are you that:
the leaves are dry, brittle and discoloured [-5. .5]? 4

How certain are you that:
the plant's environment is dry and warm [-5. .5]? why

The proposition that
the plant's environment is dry and warm

is needed in order to establish the certainty of the current goal:
the plant has been attacked by red spider mites.

A positive answer makes the goal somewhat more likely,
A negative answer makes it somewhat less likely.

Now please re-answer the question
How certain are you that:
the plant's environment is dry and warm [-5. .5]? why

The proposition that
the plant has been attacked by red spider mites

is needed in order to establish the certainty of the goal:
the plant has been attacked by an insect pest.
~~
```

Fig. 1.6 'Why' justification in expert system dialogue.

1.7.2 Limitations of mechanical justification

This form of justification is essentially a form of tracing of the mechanical reasoning process. It is particularly valuable to the developer of an expert system, when comparing the actual conclusions reached by the system with those anticipated, in the process of 'knowledge engineering' described in Chapter 4. However if, as has already been suggested, the mechanical reasoning strategy does not reflect that used by human problem solvers, 'why' justification is less helpful to end users. Clancey (1983) found this in trying to adapt the MYCIN knowledge base for teaching medical diagnosis, and concluded that it was necessary to augment explicitly the judgemental rules with a richer model of the underlying medical knowledge.

1.8 CONCLUSION

We started the chapter declining to give a definition of an expert system, saying that such a definition would be meaningless without supporting description and explanation, and that there is not sufficient agreement about what an expert system is. The three examples we looked at: MYCIN, PROSPECTOR and XCON, were all applied to areas of professional or technical expertise. They all solved difficult problems, but not always problems of the same kind. MYCIN and PROSPECTOR tackled what might be called classification problems, but XCON's task was design within constraints. We also noted that the task on its own was not a sufficient condition for a program to be described as an expert system, citing examples of programs using different techniques to tackle similar problems. Having described a number of examples, we then turned to the construction and operation of expert systems, describing four characteristics of their structure and operation.

SUMMARY
Chapter 1

Definitions of expert systems vary, focusing on the domain of application, the level of performance and the manner in which advice is given to a user. If any of these is regarded as a necessary part of the definition of an expert system, it excludes some system that has been so described.

Well-known examples of expert systems include MYCIN which advised on the diagnosis and treatment of bacterial infections, PROSPECTOR which assisted in interpreting geological data to predict the existence of valuable mineral deposits, and XCON which could design a computer configuration to match a customer's requirements.

Problems like medical diagnosis have been tackled computationally by other means, particularly involving statistics and information retrieval techniques. Other classes of interactive computer system should not be confused with expert systems.

Expert systems can also be characterized by their internal structure and operational features. These include explicit representation of domain knowledge, a general-purpose inference mechanism providing the only procedural mechanism, provision for reasoning with uncertainty, and run-time explanation for the user.

The most common way to represent domain knowledge is by a set of production rules, each of which has two components: a test or premise, and a conclusion or action.

As the production rules do not contain control information, the inference mechanism requires a strategy for selecting and applying the rules in a particular case.

Two alternatives are backward and forward chaining.

Many expert system problems deal with evidence that is uncertain, and with rules that are unreliable and based on the subjective judgement of an expert informant. The inference mechanism requires some certainty calculus that takes account of the weighted certainties of evidence in deriving that of the conclusions reached.

Three forms of certainty calculus are: fuzzy logic, subjective Bayesian reasoning, and a certainty factor combination scheme used in the MYCIN expert system.

Another distinctive feature of expert systems that distinguishes them from other interactive computer applications is their ability to justify their conclusions by generating explanations from the knowledge base.

A straightforward way of producing justification in a backward chaining system traces backwards down the stack of goals. More sophisticated systems use a more complex representation of domain knowledge to relate justification to underlying principles.

EXERCISES AND TOPICS FOR DISCUSSION Chapter 1

E1.1 What professions are susceptible to expert systems? Would such systems replace the professionals or enhance their competence?

E1.2 What aspects of computer system development do you think would benefit from the provision of an expert system?

E1.3 If you have access to a software package for developing an expert system, prepare and test a knowledge base for identifying birds by characteristics such as apparent size, flight pattern, habitat, colours, markings, time of year, shape of beak, food and feeding strategy. Use one of the many bird-spotters' guides as a source of information. Exploit the facilities provided by the software to give likely conclusions when incomplete information is supplied.

E1.4 Consider a specific computer utility such as an electronic mail system or a document preparation system, and decide whether an expert system is a feasible and useful way of providing help for end users.

2

APPRECIATION OF PROLOG

This chapter is devoted to a consideration of the distinctive features of the Prolog programming language, particularly those that render it appropriate for developing knowledge-based applications. (In later chapters we shall make reference to Prolog where matters of implementation are discussed.)

We begin by introducing the flavour of declarative programming (programming by assertion and query) in Prolog. The way Prolog differs from other languages in its approach to control structures is examined. We then review the way lists, structures and graphs are treated.

2.1 WHY PROLOG?

Prolog is a language developed in the early 1970s in several centres: Marseilles, Waterloo (Canada), Edinburgh and Imperial College, London. It is particularly popular in Europe, but is also associated with the Japanese 5th Generation Computer Project. It is a language that is particularly associated with IKBS for two reasons.

Firstly its intellectual roots are in automated theorem proving, a basic technique in AI. The theorem prover replaces almost all of what in other languages are described as 'control structures'. Secondly by packaging the theorem prover with a conversational interpreter, input/output and flexible data structuring facilities, a powerful general-purpose language has been created.

An important feature that Prolog shares with Lisp, still the major AI language, is the use of lists as the major data structure. Both languages differ from conventional languages such as Pascal in supporting the list as a data type in its own right with built-in, high-level operations on lists. By contrast, in other languages the programmer must synthesize lists and other structures from lower-level components and write supporting procedures for storage management as well as input and output. None of this is necessary in either Lisp or Prolog. Each has a notation for expressing lists directly, making it easy for the programmer to inspect the data structures during program development, a particularly important feature in the context of a prototyping approach.

A feature of Prolog not shared by Lisp is its 'declarative' nature. In this style of programming, instead of designing an algorithm, the problem specification is written as a set of facts and rules, which the theorem prover applies as needed to solve the problem. To underline the distinctive nature of this approach, Kowalski wrote a paper entitled 'Algorithm = Logic + Control' to contrast with Wirth's 'Algorithms + Data Structures = Programs'.

Nondeterministic computation is a further feature of Prolog that is relevant to some IKBS applications. It occurs when a selected rule turns out not to have been correct or useful in reaching a solution, and alternatives are tried. It is implemented in Prolog by a general **back-tracking** mechanism, although a parallel mode of execution could serve equally well for pure logic programs. We shall examine nondeterministic parsing as an example in Chapter 6.

As a by-product of these powerful mechanisms, it is also possible for items in tables and databases (including virtual databases) within the Prolog program to be accessed directly without the need to code search routines.

2.2 PROGRAMMING BY ASSERTION AND QUERY

Prolog provides a simple model of computation as data processing where the essential operations are assertion of new data and query of items in the database. The term 'database' refers to the user's workspace in an invocation of Prolog, and not to an external database controlled by a database management system. On entering Prolog, this database is initially empty, and the user is in query mode. Query mode is one of two modes of interaction with Prolog; the other is consult mode. In query mode the user can query the database or evaluate predefined predicates on constants. In consult mode, the system reads new assertions to add to the database. The user at the terminal and external files can both be consulted.

2.2.1 Interacting with Prolog

Different prompts are given by the system to show the mode it is currently in. Unfortunately these vary from one Prolog system to another, but in C-Prolog and several others the prompts are

| ?- for query mode, and | for consult mode.

Prolog always starts up in query mode.

As Prolog initially has no facts stored in its working memory or database, we should not expect answers to any questions. (There are, however, several built-in evaluable predicates, some of which we shall discuss below). To add new facts, we first go into consult mode using the predefined predicate 'consult' with the argument 'user':

| ?- consult (user).

Prolog then gives the consult mode prompt:

|

and waits for the user to input a **clause**. A simple clause consists of a **functor** followed by a sequence of arguments separated by commas. A functor in mathematics is the name of a function, and Prolog clauses are written in the notation of mathematical functions. (It should be noted, however, that Prolog clauses are not evaluated in the same way as a function written in Pascal, say). The following are all instances of clauses:

person (john).
male (john).
age (tim, 5).
address (john, 5, railway_cuttings, east_cheam).

The functors are respectively 'person', 'male', 'age' and 'address'. The clauses have 1, 1, 2 and 4 arguments respectively. In simple clauses being asserted into the database it is usual for all the arguments to be constants, either atoms or integers. Atoms, or non-numeric constants, may comprise

a string of lower-case letters (may also include underscores),

a string of one or more non-alphanumeric characters, or

any string of characters enclosed in single quotes.

Note that if we want to write a proper name as an atom, we must not start it with the customary initial capital letter.

The meaning of facts asserted in clauses is up to the user, and is not in any way accessible to Prolog, but the customary convention is to interpret the functor as a predicate that is true for the argument(s).

We shall assert the third of the above examples:

| age (tim, 5).

|^Duser consulted 12 bytes 0.016667 sec.

Note that all assertions must be terminated with a ".". Prolog then gives the consult mode prompt ready for the user to assert more clauses. In the example, we did not wish to add any more assertions, choosing instead to return to query mode. We signal this by typing control-D. (The character used may vary from one Prolog environment to another.)

Back in query mode, we are able to ask a question. Corresponding to the English question: 'Is Tim aged 5?', we type

| ?- age (tim, 5).

Note that the question has exactly the same form as the fact that was asserted. Prolog attempts to *match* the query with facts asserted in the database. It succeeds and answers 'yes', before displaying the query mode prompt again. If we ask if Tim is 6, Prolog answers 'no'. The whole 'conversation' from the stage of entering Prolog is shown in Fig. 2.1.

```
wjb > prolog
C-Prolog version 1.5
| ?- consult (user).
| age (tim, 5).
|^Duser consulted 12 bytes 0.016667 sec

| ?- age (tim, 5).
yes

| ?- age (tim, 6).

no

| ?-
```

Fig. 2.1 Sample conversation with Prolog.

2.2.2 Variable queries

All queries are eventually answered either 'yes' or 'no' by Prolog, but simple yes/no queries are ones where all the arguments are constants.

More usefully, it is possible to ask Prolog 'open' questions, that begin with 'who', 'what', 'which' and so on in English. With our existing database, we can ask 'What age is Tim?'. In Prolog this is:

| ?- age (tim, A).

and the response by Prolog is to give us a value for A, from a matching clause in the database. Generally, a variable can match any constant.

When a query containing one or more variable arguments is answered with instances of the variable(s), the cursor is left at the end of the line waiting for the user to 'accept' or 'reject' the answer. In the example, the answer has been accepted. The idea of rejecting an answer will be explained below.

Queries with negative answers

Suppose we have asserted the fact 'language (prolog)', meaning 'Prolog is a language', but no other facts about languages. If we ask

   | ?- language (basic).

the answer will be 'no'. Quite reasonably, you may say. But the reason it says 'no' is that it has not been told explicitly that Basic is a language. (Note that we had to type 'basic' instead of 'Basic', since it is a constant.)

This is not the normal way we treat negation. If you were asked 'Is Colog a language?', the most reasonable answer to give would be 'Not as far as I am aware', or 'I don't know'. In Prolog, there is no difference in meaning between 'I don't know' and 'no'. This way of handling negation is variously referred to as the 'negation as failure' convention and the 'closed world assumption'. In the former phrase, we mean that if Prolog fails to find the queried assertion in the database, it is reported to be false. In the latter phrase, we are referring to the rationale behind the convention, that in databases, we normally make the assumption that the database has complete information regarding the entities in the closed world it models. In an organization, it is reasonable to conclude that if no record of Machiavelli is present in the corporate payroll database, then Machiavelli is not an employee of the organization.

Queries with multiple answers

In the clauses listed below, each can be read as saying that the argument 'is a' language.

   | ?- consult (user).
   | language (cobol).
   | language (lisp).
   | language (fortran).
   | language (prolog).
   | language (english).
   | language(welsh).
   | ^Duser consulted 196 bytes 0.183334 sec.

   | ?-

As in our previous examples about the age of Tim, we can ask both closed (yes/no) and open questions about languages. We have already seen what happens when we ask closed questions, such as 'language (prolog)' and 'language (basic)'.

Since in our database, there is more than one instance that matches L, the open question *language (L)* has not one but several possible answers. What does Prolog do? The first answer is reported, as shown in the dialogue below, and the cursor rests at the end of the response line. As in our previous variable queries, Prolog allows the user to 'reject' this answer, by typing ";" or accept it by typing carriage return. In the former case, Prolog will attempt to find further instantiations of L. The user can find all instances, by rejecting each in turn. After the last successful match, the interpreter will say 'no'. This does not mean that the answers already given were incorrect, simply that there are no *further* matches in the database.

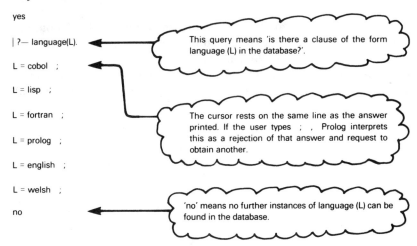

yes

| ?— language(L).

L = cobol ;

L = lisp ;

L = fortran ;

L = prolog ;

L = english ;

L = welsh ;

no

This query means 'is there a clause of the form language (L) in the database?'.

The cursor rests on the same line as the answer printed. If the user types ; , Prolog interprets this as a rejection of that answer and request to obtain another.

'no' means no further instances of language (L) can be found in the database.

Fig. 2.2   Multiple answers to a variable query.

2.2.3   Prolog and 'relational' databases

Prolog's internal database can simulate a relational database. In the latter, conceptual entities are represented by a series of 'tuples', one for each occurrence. A tuple stores a value for each attribute of an entity. For example, an entity 'part' in a stock-control database may have the attributes part_number, description and quantity. A part tuple can be entered directly into the Prolog database as an assertion:

part (1020343, camshaft, 2).

The entity type is indicated by using its name as the functor in the Prolog clause.

The part table (or *relation* using relational database terminology) comprises all the Prolog clauses with 'part' as functor and three arguments. With these in the Prolog database, it is simple to pose queries based on any of the arguments' values.

For example

| ?- part (Partno, Description, 0).

lists all the parts with a zero stock balance, and

| ?- part (Partno, distributor, Qty).

retrieves the Part number and quantity in stock for all parts described as 'distributor'.

The power of relational databases lies in the ability to answer queries involving tuples of more than one type, where the sharing of values of corresponding attributes indicates the occurrence of a relationship between the real-world entities.

Prolog queries using variables can establish instances of relationships between entities in the way that a relational database can 'join' different relations or tables together. We can represent a database of information about projects and staff in a software house by sets of Prolog facts of the forms: project (Projname, Lang_used) and employee (Name, Lang_known). Instances of such a database might include the following:

project (payroll, cobol).	employee (mary, cobol).
project (network, pascal).	employee (mary, ada).
project (sdi, ada).	employee (john, pascal).
project (poem, snobol).	employee (john, ada).
project (ikbs, prolog).	employee (anna, prolog).
	employee (ada, pascal).
	employee (simon, snobol).
	employee (bill, cobol).
	employee (bill, prolog).

With this database, we can use queries that incorporate conjunctions of clauses (using "," as the conjunction operator) to establish potential relationship between the two types of entity. For example:

   | ?- project (sdi, Lang), employee (Name, Lang).

will result in a report of those employees whose language knowledge matches the language requirement for the star wars project, whatever that language happens to be.

   | ?- project (Projname, Lang), employee (simon, Lang).

will tell us which projects, if any, Simon can be assigned to.

2.2.4 Built-in evaluable predicates

Several built-in predicates are provided in Prolog for the convenience of the programmer. One we have met already is 'consult'. Others are provided to do things such as evaluate arithmetic expressions, input and output with external files, and convert from one type of data structure to another. The following conversation shows how two such predicates may be evaluated in queries.

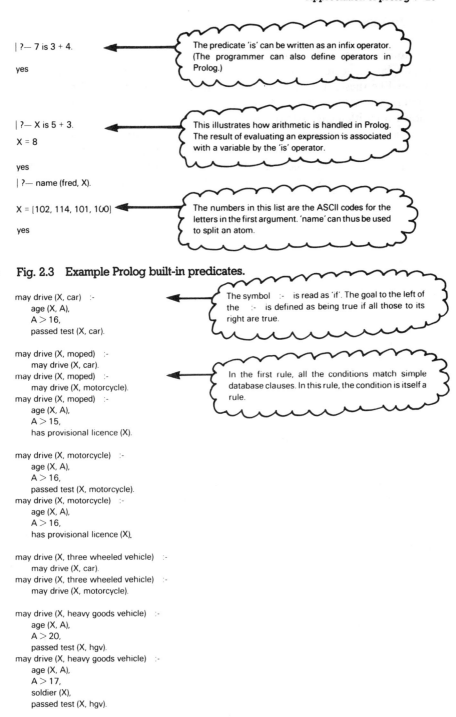

| ?— 7 is 3 + 4.

yes

> The predicate 'is' can be written as an infix operator. (The programmer can also define operators in Prolog.)

| ?— X is 5 + 3.

X = 8

yes

> This illustrates how arithmetic is handled in Prolog. The result of evaluating an expression is associated with a variable by the 'is' operator.

| ?— name (fred, X).

X = [102, 114, 101, 100]

yes

> The numbers in this list are the ASCII codes for the letters in the first argument. 'name' can thus be used to split an atom.

Fig. 2.3 Example Prolog built-in predicates.

may drive (X, car) :-
    age (X, A),
    A > 16,
    passed test (X, car).

> The symbol :- is read as 'if'. The goal to the left of the :- is defined as being true if all those to its right are true.

may drive (X, moped) :-
    may drive (X, car).
may drive (X, moped) :-
    may drive (X, motorcycle).
may drive (X, moped) :-
    age (X, A),
    A > 15,
    has provisional licence (X).

> In the first rule, all the conditions match simple database clauses. In this rule, the condition is itself a rule.

may drive (X, motorcycle) :-
    age (X, A),
    A > 16,
    passed test (X, motorcycle).
may drive (X, motorcycle) :-
    age (X, A),
    A > 16,
    has provisional licence (X).

may drive (X, three wheeled vehicle) :-
    may drive (X, car).
may drive (X, three wheeled vehicle) :-
    may drive (X, motorcycle).

may drive (X, heavy goods vehicle) :-
    age (X, A),
    A > 20,
    passed test (X, hgv).
may drive (X, heavy goods vehicle) :-
    age (X, A),
    A > 17,
    soldier (X),
    passed test (X, hgv).

Fig. 2.4 Prolog rules for entitlement to drive

2.3 RULES

The above examples have illustrated how Prolog may be used as a query and update language for a simple database. In addition to answering direct queries like these, it is also possible to make inferences beyond the factual database if rules have been added. As an example, a series of rules are listed below for entitlement to drive various vehicles. Generally speaking, there is a lower age limit for each class of vehicle, and also a requirement of either passing a test or holding a provisional licence. Being able to drive some types of vehicle gives entitlement to drive others. Mopeds and three-wheeled vehicles are examples, where anyone entitled to drive a car or a motorcycle is also permitted to drive these vehicles.

```
/* database of facts */

age (julie, 20).
age (john, 18).
age (simon, 16).
age (james, 21).
age (jane, 18).

passed_test (julie, car).
passed_test (john, motorcycle).
passed_test (john, hgv).
passed_test (james, hgv).

soldier (john).

has_provisional_licence (simon).
has_provisional_licence (jane).
```

Fig. 2.5 Sample fact database to be used with rules in Fig. 2.4.

Figure 2.6 shows several queries made against the driving rules database. We start with yes/no questions, where the arguments are given as constants. Then we move on to questions of the form 'What may X drive?' and finally to those of the form 'Who may drive an X?'. The reader may verify that Prolog has made the correct inferences according to the rules and facts given.

2.3.1 Unification

'Unification' is the name that is given to the powerful parameter substitution process that Prolog uses whenever it matches a goal with a fact or head of a rule in the database. Variables and constants in queries and database clauses may be unified or matched as follows:

- A constant matches the same constant.
- A variable matches a constant and becomes **instantiated** to that constant.

- A variable matches another variable that is not yet instantiated. The two variables then **share**, and as soon as one of them subsequently matches a constant, they are both simultaneously instantiated to it.

The above rules also apply when a constant or variable is matched to a *part* of

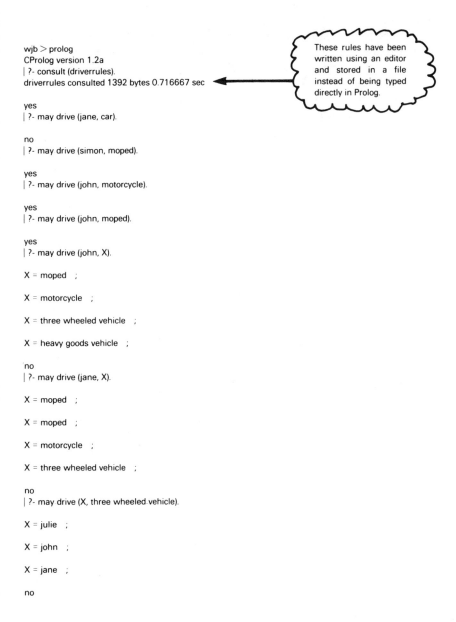

```
wjb > prolog
CProlog version 1.2a
| ?- consult (driverrules).
driverrules consulted 1392 bytes 0.716667 sec

yes
| ?- may drive (jane, car).

no
| ?- may drive (simon, moped).

yes
| ?- may drive (john, motorcycle).

yes
| ?- may drive (john, moped).

yes
| ?- may drive (john, X).

X = moped   ;

X = motorcycle   ;

X = three wheeled vehicle   ;

X = heavy goods vehicle   ;

no
| ?- may drive (jane, X).

X = moped   ;

X = moped   ;

X = motorcycle   ;

X = three wheeled vehicle   ;

no
| ?- may drive (X, three wheeled vehicle).

X = julie   ;

X = john   ;

X = jane   ;

no
```

These rules have been written using an editor and stored in a file instead of being typed directly in Prolog.

Fig. 2.6   Answers to queries with rules.

a list or structure. Lists and structures in Prolog are both discussed below under the heading 'Data Structuring'.

The second and third rules for unification resemble the parameter substitution process in a conventional procedural or functional language, but are more powerful. The arguments in the head of a rule are the 'formal parameters' whereas those of the goal are the 'actual parameters'. In a conventional language, the usage of the parameters as input or output parameters is determined by the procedural statements. In Prolog, it is possible to use a given parameter as an input parameter in one invocation and as an output parameter in another. For example, the predefined predicate *name*, illustrated in Fig. 2.3, where it was used to input an atom and output a list of its character codes, can also be used to input a list of character codes and output the corresponding atom, as shown below:

| ?- name (Word, [99, 97, 98]).

Word = cab

2.3.2 Backtracking

In answering the query 'may_drive (john, heavy_goods_vehicle)', there are ten *may_drive* clauses in Fig. 2.4 with which Prolog can attempt to match the query. The first one that matches is the ninth, with X instantiated (or bound) to 'john'. The first condition in the right-hand side of this rule matches the second *age* clause, binding the variable A to the integer constant 18. The second condition fails, since 18 is not greater than 20. The first rule, then, has failed as a whole, but the goal of proving that john may_drive a heavy_goods_ vehicle has not, since there is an alternative rule. When the goal *18 > 20* fails, Prolog first attempts to resatisfy the goal *age (john, X)*, but there are no further matches with john as first argument. **Backtracking** then proceeds further to the left, to the head of the rule.

Since there is another rule, Prolog attempts to use it in an alternative proof of the goal. With this last rule, the binding *X = john* is made again, the goal *age (john, A)* is reattempted, with the same result, *A = 18*. This time, the next condition, *soldier (john)* is satisfied directly by a fact in the database, as also is the *passed test* clause. Figure 2.7 shows a trace of the backtracking involved in answering the above query as a 'search tree'.

Whenever Prolog fails to prove a condition in the right-hand side of a rule, instead of immediately giving up, it attempts to see if there is any other way to satisfy the parent goal. It first attempts to see if there is any other way to satisfy the goal to the left of the failed goal. If it in turn cannot be resatisfied, the goal to its left is retried. If a failed goal is the first condition in a rule, Prolog's backtracking mechanism attempts any further rules with a matching head.

In summary, we can say that a goal in the right-hand side of a rule.

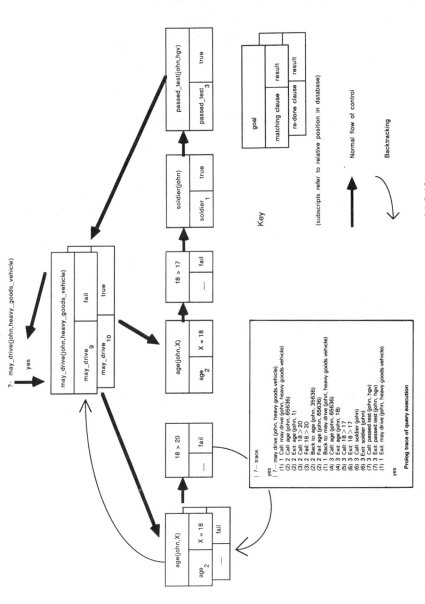

Fig. 2.7 Backtracking in answering the query 'may_drive (john, heavy_goods_vehicle)'.

reports success to its right neighbour (or if there is no right neighbour, to the parent goal).

reports failure to its left neighbour (or parent goal).

Prolog provides a tracing facility that reports each time a goal is CALLed, PROVED, FAILed or REDOne. It is especially useful in learning about the backtracking process and is illustrated in the box in Fig. 2.7.

2.4   Prolog as a practical programming language

Input and output

Prolog always reports instantiations of variables when a query has been evaluated, but serious programs written in Prolog require input and output at the discretion of the programmer. Prolog has a range of defined input and output procedures that can be invoked as goals. The procedure *write*, can be called to output the Prolog term given as its argument, and the goal *nl* with no arguments sends a carriage return. *Read* can be used to input a Prolog term, with the user having to terminate the input with a period and carriage return. Other predicates exist for unbuffered character input and file input/output. Procedures like these are invoked for their practical effects, and do not have a logical sense.

Control structures

The examples of queries involving both facts and rules illustrate most of what in other languages would have been discussed under the heading of 'control structures'. In a rule for example, the various conjuncts are applied in sequence. The use of alternative rules is the Prolog way of dealing with selection. (It is also possible to use ";" as an explicit disjunction operator in the body of a rule.) We haven't said anything about iteration, and where it is called for in our examples, we have up to now forced the user to implement it manually. There are several ways of doing those things in Prolog that in other languages could be done with iteration.

Repeat ... fail

One method is to deliberately force the interpreter to backtrack. This is done by the predicate *fail* which always fails. *fail* is like the ";" at query level, but it can be incorporated into the body of a rule. To get Prolog to iterate through the previous actions, it is necessary to use a further predicate *repeat*, as shown in Fig. 2.8 below:

```
| forever :-
|    repeat,
|       write ('forever'), nl,
|          fail.
|
| ?- forever.
forever
forever
forever
^Cforever
forever
Action (h for help):
a

[execution aborted]

| ?-
```

Fig. 2.8   Infinite iteration with repeat and fail.

Controlled iteration

Figure 2.9 shows a more controlled form of iteration. There are many alternative ways of doing this. The present example makes use of the **disjunction** operator, ";" in the right-hand side of a rule.

```
language (cobol).
language (lisp).
language (fortran).
language (prolog).
language (english).
language (welsh).

until:-
   repeat,
       (language (L),
       write (L), write ('is a language'), nl,
       fail
       ;
       write ('No (more) languages'),
       nl
       ).

| ?- until.
cobol is a language
lisp is a language
fortran is a language
prolog is a language
english is a language
welsh is a language
No (more) languages

yes
| ?-
```

Fig. 2.9   Controlled iteration with repeat ... fail.

Each time a *language* (*L*) clause is found, the *fail* goal causes failure, and so backtracking returns to *repeat*, which succeeds, generating new goals from the clauses to its 'right'. When no further solutions are found, the first disjunct fails and the second succeeds. As the second disjunct does not contain a *fail* goal, the right-hand side of the *until* rule is finally satisfied.

2.4.1 The cut

The cut, written "!", is a special goal whose sole purpose is to remove alternative backtracking paths. Its behaviour is as follows:

- The cut always succeeds when it is called.

- If the goals to its right all succeed, the cut has no effect.

- If backtracking takes place among the goals to its right, but success is attained without backtracking into the cut, it has no effect.

- If the goals to the right of the cut fail, upon backtracking into the cut, the current goal and its parent goal both fail, and no further solutions are tried.

One use of the cut is to implement reasoning by default. If we have some clauses about the properties of animals, such as:

```
skin (fish, scaly).
skin (mammal, furry).
skin (reptile, smooth).
skin (bird, feathery).

/* exceptions */
skin (dolphin, smooth).
skin (human, smooth).

/* general rule */
skin (Animal, Texture) :-   isa (Animal, Class),
                            skin (Class, Texture).

isa (mouse, mammal).
isa (dog, mammal).
isa (human, mammal).
isa (cod, fish).
isa (lizard, reptile).
isa (robin, bird).
isa (dolphin, mammal).
```

and we ask about the skin type of humans we will get the answers:

| ?- skin (human, smooth).

yes

| ?- skin (human, S).

S = smooth.

| ?- skin (human, furry).

yes

| ?- skin (human, S).

S = smooth;

S = furry

The first two answers are correct. The third and last are not. Prolog produced these by backtracking and using the general rule. To stop the general rule from being applied where we have an exception, we use the cut to remove alternative solutions. We rewrite the exception clauses as rules:

```
/* exceptions */

skin (dolphin, S) :- !, S = smooth.
skin (human, S) :- !, S = smooth.
```

Here, if we have the goal *skin (human, furry)*, the head of the rule is matched successfully, so the cut in the tail succeeds. Control passes to the goal to its right, *S = smooth*. This goal fails, since the binding for S was 'furry'. Backtracking then takes place, into the cut, resulting in a failure of the parent goal *skin (human, furry)*.

The cut is sometimes also used simply to save fruitless backtracking which will not produce alternative solutions anyway, in other words solely for efficiency.

2.4.2 Collecting sets of instantiations

If instantiations of variables are wanted for further processing, then it is possible to collect them together into a single list, and at the top level this will succeed only once. There are two predicates predefined in some Prologs (but also defined in Clocksin and Mellish, 1984) for this: *setof* and *bagof*. *Setof* provides a list of all unique solutions to a variable instantiation whereas *bagof* gives all solutions. To form a set of all languages known to the database, we would ask for:

| ?- setof (L, language (L), Langset).

and Prolog would respond:

```
L =  0
Langset = [fortran, cobol, pascal, prolog, english, welsh]

yes
| ?-
```

We shall discuss shortly the Prolog list notation in its own right. The first argument in the setof goal identifies the variable whose instances are to be collected. The second is the goal clause that is to be matched against assertions in the database, and the third is the variable that serves as the output parameter for the results. The first parameter is of particular importance if the goal clause has more than one argument. For example, if we wanted to know the names of all the employees in the staff database (where an example clause was 'employee (mary, pascal)'), but not their languages, we could ask for:

```
| ?- setof (N, employee (N,_), Namelist).
```

Note that the underscore in the above example represents an **anonymous variable** whose place we must mark in a goal, but whose value is not wanted. (It is rather like 'FILLER' in COBOL).

2.5 RECURSION

Ancestry in a family is often cited as an instance of a recursive relationship. There are many such relationships that occur in other contexts, e.g. hierarchies in organizations, clauses and phrases in sentences, components and sub-assemblies in manufactured artifacts. A software module hierarchy is an example of the last. The relation between a module and its immediate constituents can be modelled in the database by a series of assertions such as 'calls (a, b)'. Instances of called programs, like b, may themselves call other modules, which may in turn have component modules of their own, down to an arbitrary depth. The relationship 'has_component' thus applies both to directly and indirectly called component modules. It can be defined as:

```
has_component (A,B) :-
    calls (A,B).
has_component (A,B) :-
    calls (A,C),
    has_component (C,B).
```

This rule can determine whether a given module is used in a particular program, with a goal such as:

```
| ?- has_component (main, getchar).
```

or to produce a list of all components of a given program, using setof:

| ?- setof (Module, has_component (main, Module), Module_set).

Whilst recursive relationships can be recorded in unit clauses such as the 'calls' facts, recursive rules are more frequently used with structured data, for example lists.

2.6 DATA STRUCTURING

2.6.1 Lists

We have already met examples of Prolog lists twice. Near the beginning of the chapter, the built-in predicate 'name' produced the list of ASCII codes corresponding to an atom as a list, and the 'setof' predicate produced a list too.

Lists can also be arguments in rules written by the programmer. To write such rules, it is necessary to be able to access the component parts of a list separately. As we want any such rules to generalize to lists of any length, a list is defined recursively. It is considered to be a head component followed by a tail, which is another list. (For comparison, Pascal does not recognize a list as a type, but instead allows the programmer to define a list pointer as a pointer to an object containing a similar pointer.)

In addition to the square bracket for delimiting the list and the commas for separating the elements, there is one further notational device: "|". This symbol shows where the list is to be split into a head and a tail. At this point we need an illustration. Consider a database of colours where we assert just a single list of all colours instead of several separate facts:

colours ([red, orange, yellow, green, blue, indigo, violet]).

The problem now is to tell whether a given atom is a known colour, e.g. ?-colour (green), or ?-colour (purple). What we are asking is whether each is a *member* of the set of colours, i.e.

colour (C) :-
    colours (Colourset),
    member (C, Colourset).

In the head of the rule defining the member relationship, we show how the list may be 'dismembered' using a list pattern: [Head|Tail]. In the body of this rule, we may subsequently use the variable Head to refer to the first element of whatever list has been supplied as an actual parameter, and Tail to refer to a list made up of the remaining elements. Using this notation the rule for membership can be written:

member (Element, [Head|Tail]) :-
    Head = Element.

```
member (Element, [Head|Tail]) :-
    member (Element, Tail).
```

In the first definition, we deal with the special case that the element is the same as the first component of the list. In the second definition, an element is a member of it is a member of the tail (a recursive definition).

These definitions can be abbreviated. In the first definition, we don't need a tail for the rule, since we can test whether Head = Element by using the same variable in both positions in the goal: member (Element, [Element|Tail]). Furthermore, we are not interested in what the tail is if the element has matched the head. The latter point also applies to the second definition, where we are not interested in what the head was. (We would not have used the second definition if the first had succeeded.) The tersest form of the rule to determine set membership, using anonymous variables, is thus:

```
member (M, [M|_]).
member (M, [_|T]) :-
    member (M, T).
```

In the list patterns in both definitions, a list must have at least one element in order to match (the tail can be the empty list). In other rules applied to lists, we may need to allow explicitly for special cases such as the empty list, as in the following procedure to determine the length of a list:

```
listsize ([],0).          /* An empty list is of length 0 */
listsize ([_|T], N) :-
    listsize (T, N1),
    N is N1 + 1.
```

Often, the limiting condition for a recursively defined operation on lists involves the empty list as it has in this example.

There are no built-in definitions in most Prolog implementations for the common list-processing operations (although there are operations to convert atoms and structures to lists and vice-versa). The programmer must therefore build up a library of utilities. This is not too difficult as they are to be found in textbooks such as Clocksin and Mellish (1984), and in the Coelh, Cotta and Pereira (1982) collection of illustrative Prolog programs.

2.7 STRUCTURES

In the same way that Lisp has a uniform notation for programs and data structures, it is possible to use the same notation to structure data as that for Prolog clauses. A functor with a bracketed list of arguments is called a 'structure' in Prolog when it is considered as data. We could use structures in the company database example from the beginning of the chapter, for example:

employee (name (john, smith), age (28), dept (scientific), location (brighton))

This use of structures resembles records in conventional data procesing, but they can also be used to build more sophisticated knowledge representations like frames. Structures are more versatile than this example shows, however, since in a rule, both

employe (A,B,C,D)   and
employee (N(O,P),Q,R,S)

can match the given clause. It is possible to use structures to implement a recursive tree structure. We will not give detailed illustrations of the use of structures here, since they are used to build parse trees in Chapter 6 where we analyse natural language sentences in Prolog.

2.7.1 Graphs

Graphs are frequently encountered in IKBS. For example, semantic nets (see Chapter 3) are used to give a visual representation of complex relationships. Here we shall restrict our attention to general observations about graph representation and search.

For example, we can represent geographical information as a graph. An abstract model of part of the rail network in northern England is shown in Fig. 2.10.

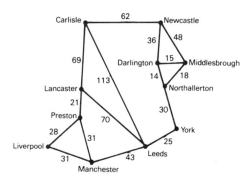

Fig. 2.10   Graph representing a railway network.

The numbers shown beside each edge on the graph represent the approximate distance in track-miles between the two stations at either end of the edge.

A graph such as this can easily be stored and manipulated in Prolog. Each edge in the graph is represented by a unit clause whose arguments are the labels for the nodes (and, if needed, for the edge). The clauses below are examples.

/* data */

line (carlisle, newcastle, 62).
line (newcastle, middlesbrough, 48).
line (newcastle, darlington, 36).
line (darlington, middlesbrough, 15).
line (darlington, northallerton, 14).
line (northallerton, york, 30).
line (york, leeds, 25).
line (leeds, manchester, 43).
line (manchester, liverpool, 31).
line (liverpool, preston, 28).
line (manchester, preston, 31).
line (preston, lancaster, 21).
line (leeds, lancaster, 70).
line (leeds, carlisle, 113).
line (lancaster, carlisle, 69).

By default, such clauses can represent a directed graph with the direction shown conventionally by the order of the node arguments. An undirected graph can be represented either by asserting a pair of clauses for each edge or else by a general rule showing that any edge connects both nodes in the opposite direction to the one stated. The latter is illustrated by the two rules below:

link (A,B,D) :-   link (A,B,D) :-
   line (A,B,D).   line (B,A,D).

The problem addressed by this example is to establish if there is a route on the network between two given places, and if so, what is the total distance. A Prolog rule capable of answering the query 'What is the route from A to B and the total distance?', for example:

| ?- route (manchester, newcastle, Route, Distance).

is given below:

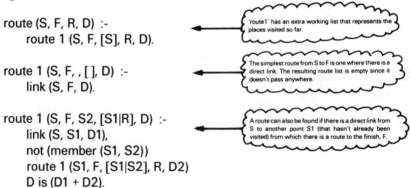

route (S, F, R, D) :-
   route 1 (S, F, [S], R, D).

'route1' has an extra working list that represents the places visited so far.

route 1 (S, F, , [ ], D) :-
   link (S, F, D).

The simplest route from S to F is one where there is a direct link. The resulting route list is empty since it doesn't pass anywhere.

route 1 (S, F, S2, [S1|R], D) :-
   link (S, S1, D1),
   not (member (S1, S2))
   route 1 (S1, F, [S1|S2], R, D2)
   D is (D1 + D2).

A route can also be found if there is a direct link from S to another point S1 (that hasn't already been visited) from which there is a route to the finish, F.

A route exists from a starting point, S to a finish point, F, where there is either a direct link between the two points, or else a link from S to another point, S1 that has a route to F. The third parameter of route 1 maintains a list of places already visited, and the test *member (S1, S2)* ensures that the route doesn't go over the same ground more than once. The distances are accumulated in D.

2.7.2 Nondeterministic programming

In processing both lists and graphs, it is common to deliberately exploit Prolog's general backtracking mechanism. A search process is termed **nondeterministic** if the execution path cannot be predicted. Often a procedure that can be specified algorithmically can be defined more succinctly as a nondeterministic computation using a general backtracking mechanism such as that of Prolog. As an example, let us consider the 'search and replace' operation found in a typical text editor. A procedure to do this will take three input parameters: the input string, the search pattern and the replacement, and will produce one output parameter, the output string. It could be called as follows:

| ?- sr('an old string', 'n old', 'new', Output).

Output = a new string

Figure 2.11 gives a Prolog definition for such a procedure that operates on atoms as input and output parameters.

```
sr (Instring, Search, Replacement, Outstring) :-
    name (Instring, Inlist),
    name (Search, Searchlist),
    name (Replacement, Replist),
    append (Beginning, Ending, Inlist), /* Break Inlist into 2 */
    append (Searchlist, Remainder, Ending),
    append (Replist, Remainder, Newending), /* Build new ending */
    append (Beginning, Newending, Outlist), /* Rebuild whole list */
    name (Outstring, Outlist).
```

Fig. 2.11 Nondeterministic Search and Replace procedure.

In the tail of the *sr* rule in Fig. 2.11, there are several calls of two other Prolog procedures: *name* is built-in, but *append* is not. It defines the relationship between two lists and a list formed by appending them together. We will not examine the definition of *append* here, but note that it behaves as:

| ?- append ([f,i,r,s,t], [s,e,c,o,n,d], A).

A = [f,i,r,s,t,s,e,c,o,n,d]

| ?- append ([o,t,h,e,r], S, [o,t,h,e,r,h,a,l,f]).

S = [h,a,l,f]

| ?- append (A,B, [1,2,3]).

A = []
B = [1,2,3];

A = [1]
B = [2,3]

In *sr, append* partitions the input list of characters into three portions, *Beginning, Searchlist*, and *Remainder*. It has to be used twice to do this, since it is defined to show how a list can be partitioned in two instead of three parts. In the first call to *append* within the tail of the rule, we are asking for an arbitrary division into two components, since we do not know at what point in the list the search string begins. For any such partition, the second call to *append* may or may not find the search string at the beginning of the second part of the original string. If the second call to *append* should fail, backtracking to the first call may generate an alternative partition of the original list that might contain the search string. In the first call, *append* is used nondeterministically. The third and fourth calls to *append* are used to build up new lists, and as each invocation has two actual parameters instantiated, it is used deterministically there.

2.8 EVALUATION OF PROLOG

2.8.1 Logic programming

To begin with, in describing Prolog as a language for assertion and query of a virtual database, Prolog seemed very logical. Prolog rules stated simply a set of conditions that had to be satisfied, and there was no need to specify an algorithm to evaluate a rule – the Prolog inference mechanism handled that automatically. However, we noted that it was not possible, except by using the 'setof' predicate, to obtain multiple answers to queries in a purely logical notation. We could force Prolog to do what in other languages would be termed 'iteration' by deliberately affecting the backtracking mechanism, either at query level or within the program by using the fail and cut predicates. If either of these is used, it is not possible to give Prolog procedures a purely logical reading as a set of rules, but it is necessary to view them just like procedures in any other language. Worse, the cut and fail predicates are much lower-level control primitives than those of high-level languages and programs using them are not easily understood.

The cut can be avoided in default reasoning by explicitly expressing general cases as rules that apply when the exceptions do not, using a negated condition. *Fail* can usually be eliminated by using *setof* to collect multiple instantiations of results or recursive list processing instead of attempting to design iterative algorithms in a language that is not suited to them.

If we are adhering to the discipline of logic programming, we should also avoid writing procedures where the order of the clauses is significant. Our example rule for determining the length of a list relies on the limiting condition being tested first in each recursive invocation. (Otherwise the rule is left-recursive and its evaluation never terminates.) The solution here is to embody a condition in the tail of the general rule that the length must not be negative. In general, order-dependence can be avoided by the inclusion of negated conditions in rules.

In conclusion, Prolog is not a pure logic programming language, but the programmer can use a self-imposed restricted style of programming in Prolog that avoids the worst obscurities of the explicit control mechanisms. However a pure logic programming language would not be a very useful tool.

2.8.2 Prolog for expert systems

A rule in a production system can easily be encoded in the syntax of a Prolog rule. The observable facts of an individual case can be directly entered into the Prolog database, and a conclusion can be made a Prolog query. The query can be answered 'yes' or 'no' or with values for variables. This however is not an expert system, as it is not possible to either interactively obtain case data from the user, or for the latter to inspect the inference engine's line of reasoning or intermediate results (except through Prolog's low-level tracing facilities). However, Prolog's high-level lists and structures can represent rules as data, and the database can be used easily as the working memory for the case data, intermediate results and for the agenda of goals.

In conclusion, these features render Prolog a suitable language for developing an expert system, although not by a simple mapping of domain rules on to Prolog rules.

SUMMARY
Chapter 2

Prolog is a powerful programming language based on logic theorem proving.

Prolog is an interactive language providing two basic operations: assertion and query. From the logical point of view, assertions are axioms and queries are theorems to be proved.

The queries that can be answered include both questions that are answered 'yes' or 'no' according to whether a match can be found in the working database, and those involving variables, of which Prolog seeks to find instances.

Assertions are divided into two classes: facts and rules. A rule is a conditional assertion, showing the conditions under which its head is true. A database comprising facts and rules can be thought of as a virtual database, where facts not asserted explicitly may be inferred at query time.

The standard Prolog control mechanism is a goal-directed proof procedure that chains backwards from the user's query until it eventually reaches either asserted facts (and the query is satisfied) or fails to find matching assertions (when the query is answered negatively).

If an initial attempt to prove a rule fails, Prolog invokes a general backtracking mechanism to attempt to find an alternative proof.

The Prolog matching of variables and constants in queries and assertions is known as 'unification', and defines a much more powerful parameter substitution mechanism than other high-level languages.

Prolog provides several built-in evaluable predicates for input and output, arithmetic, data structure conversion and for influencing directly the standard control mechanism. It is therefore a practical programming language and not a pure logic theorem prover. However, once these extra-logical features are incorporated, Prolog loses some of the clarity that the declarative programming style can provide.

Arbitrarily complex data structures can be manipulated in Prolog directly, without type declarations and explicit pointer manipulation. Prolog has a special syntax for lists and structures, and unification is generalized to enable matching of variables with the components of structures. Graphs can easily be created by a series of simple assertions.

Many of the distinctive features of Prolog are of use in building expert systems and other IKBS applications, but it is not possible to map rules of a production system directly on to Prolog rules if run-time user support is required.

EXERCISES Chapter 2

E2.1 Write a set of Prolog rules that represent the rules of some organizational system you are familiar with:

for example, the conditions for passing the course you are studying, or for determining eligibility for a postgraduate grant.

E2.2 Modify (1) so that it obtains the case data by asking the user instead of relying on the database to have the relevant facts already.

E2.3 Revise (2) so that the program will allow the user to iterate through the 'consultations' on the rule set.

E2.4 Using the definition of the listsize predicate for guidance, define a rule that will return the *nth* element of a given list. For example, *nth* ([*a, short, list*], 2, *Nth*) should return *Nth* = *short*.

E2.5 Write Prolog rules to determine if a given list of integers is in ascending order.

E2.6 The route-finding rule presented above may not return the most direct route between two points. Write an enhanced route-finding program that finds alternative routes and establishes which is the shortest.

3

IKBS – KNOWLEDGE REPRESENTATION

Following the extensive consideration given to rules in the general discussion of expert systems and in Prolog, we look at how objects or entities are structured in a knowledge-base. We examine first the logical basis of knowledge representations, and then a number of the formalisms used in AI/IKBS. The formalisms considered are clausal logic, semantic networks and frames.

3.1 RULES AND OBJECTS

When we looked at expert systems as examples of knowledge based systems, we characterized them in two ways – first as a class of computer systems used in a professional context in an advisory role, and secondly as having certain structural and functional characteristics.

The most important way in which one expert system differs from another is in the application specific knowledge used. This is demonstrably so, since expert systems have been constructed for widely differing applications using the same 'inference engine', differing only in their knowledge bases.

Up to now, we have assumed that knowledge can be represented primarily as either rules or simple unconditional facts. The knowledge base comprises mostly rules, and the working database of the system contains the facts of an individual case while it is under consideration.

Production rules represent knowledge in a form that can be applied directly to a problem. A diagnostic expert system's rules deal only with diagnosis and do not represent the underlying scientific knowledge that justifies it. As such, production rules can be said to model procedures declaratively. We noted in

Chapter 1 that to provide adequate justification, an expert system should represent not only applicable diagnostic rules, but also domain principles. To do this, we require to represent objects and relationships rather than conditions and actions.

As elsewhere in computing, these two views of systems, the procedural orientation and the object orientation are both needed. As with simple programs in general, simple expert systems may be constructed with scant attention to data objects and their relationships. However, for more sophisticated applications, the representation of the rules which comprise an expert's judgemental knowledge is made more complex by the existence of multiple objects and complex relationships between them. We consider some examples:

- In XCON, a computer configuration normally includes multiple instances of many of its components.
- In an advisory system for detecting the source of oil or hazardous chemical spills and clearing them up, there are multiple major plants components as well as pipeways and drains.
- In MYCIN, the patient under consideration has several cultures taken from him at different times, each of which may contain several organisms, and in order to treat the infection, it may be necessary to prescribe several drugs each of which may interact with the others.

Any rules referring to such objects within their conditions will be invoked more than once in a typical consultation, and the rule format must be capable of reflecting this generality. We now consider in more detail the logical basis and structure of rules.

3.2 LOGIC FOR KNOWLEDGE REPRESENTATION

Up to now, we have used notations for representing facts and relationships without questioning the logical basis of the notations. We start with the assumption that any such notation is capable of translation to a more conventional logical formalism. We regard logic not so much as an alternative knowledge representation language, but rather as a basis for evaluation, exposition and comparison of the actual notations used in IKBS.

3.2.1 Propositional logic

In introducing expert systems, we introduced the basic form of the production rule, as a set of conditions related to a set of conclusions or actions, without saying anything about the structure of conditions or conclusions. Leaving aside the probabilistic nature of the rules, we have the basic rule structure:

IF conjunction of propositions THEN proposition

The operation of the inference engine in such a rule-based expert system is concerned with confirming the truth of the propositions in the conclusion part of some rule or rules. It does this by establishing the truth of the propositions in the condition part of the role by mechanically following the logical rules of inference whose schemata are shown as:

A,B |= A&B   (From A and B both separately true, the conjunction A&B is inferred)

A → B, A |= B   (From A implies B and the affirmation of A, B is inferred)

The latter rule of inference was known to medieval logicians and was named 'modus ponendo ponens' (or 'modus ponens' for short). It is the fundamental operation of a rule-based system interpreter, so some observers have described an inference engine as a 'modus ponens machine'.

Propositional logic is concerned with how the truth of complex propositions may be established from that of the atomic propositions from which they are made. Atomic propositions correspond to states of affairs, as may be described in declarative sentences in ordinary language. The principal property of a proposition in logic is that it can be true or false.

Propositions may be combined to form syntactically well-formed formulae (**wffs**) of the propositional calculus using the propositional connectives AND, OR, NOT, and IMPLIES. (There are several notational variants of these in different textbooks. Here, the symbols "&", "V", "~", and "→", respectively, will be used.) The first three of these will be recognized as the operators of Boolean algebra used in logic circuits and programming languages. The implication connective corresponds in logical notation to a variety of relationships between propositions – causation, time sequence, observed association, obligation – that are used in both everyday and scientific discourse. In 'classical' logic, each of the propositional connectives is given a precise definition, in the form of a truth table, which shows, for each connective, how the truth of a compound proposition constructed with it is related to the truth of its components. We say that a logical connective or operator is 'truth functional' if its meaning is defined in this way. The truth table for implication is:

P	Q	P → Q
T	T	T
T	F	F
F	T	T
F	F	T

The connective whose meaning is defined according to the truth table above is referred to as 'material implication', to denote that there is nothing in the definition to require that the components are in any way related. In other words, the logical account of implication does not capture the full meaning of 'if ... then ...' or 'implies' in ordinary language. With the truth functional definition of →, the following is always a valid line of reasoning:

P |= Q → P

An instance of such reasoning is 'Since Wednesday follows Tuesday, we can conclude that if goats' entrails are green then Wednesday follows Tuesday'. Such a line of argument normally has no harmful consequences, but it serves to emphasize that in the usual use of implication, there has to be a connection of content between the component propositions.

3.2.2 Predicate logic

The chief drawback of propositional logic as a formalism for explicating the structure of reason and argument is that, in ignoring the internal structure of propositions, it fails to represent significant generalizations. For example, the implication:

If Katy is a child then she goes to school.

can be encoded as P → Q in propositional logic, where P stands for the proposition 'Katy is a child' and Q for 'Katy goes to school'. The propositional logic representation fails to capture the generality that can be expressed in English by substituting more general referring expressions for the name of an individual. For example: 'If **anyone** is a child, then **that person** goes to school.' Or, closer still to the formalism of logic,

For any individual X, if X is a child then X goes to school.

With this rephrasing, we can translate directly into symbolic form:

(∀X) [child (X) → goes_to_school (X)]

child(X)' represents the predicate 'is a child' applied to X, and 'goes_to_school(X)' represents the predicate 'goes to school' applied to X. 'X' is a **bound variable** which is in the **scope of the universal quantifier '∀X'**, which can be read 'For all X'. Without the quantifier and the scope-delimiting brackets, the implication resembles (apart from the order of antecedent and consequent) a Prolog rule, such as those we have met in Chapter 2. This is no accident, since the Prolog language is explicitly intended to embody the formalism of logic within an automatic deduction system. In Prolog, all rules are understood to be universally quantified, so the quantifier symbol is not used. In comparison with predicate logic, this is a restriction, (to which we return in the evaluation of clausal logic as a knowledge representation formalism below), since there is a further quantifier in predicate logic, the **existential quantifier,** ∃. The existential quantifier, read as 'For some', denotes that there are some (at least one) occurrences for which the predicates within its scope are true. For example, if 'black (X)' denotes that X is black, and 'swan (X)' denotes that X is a swan, '(∃X) [swan (X) & black (X)]' means that some swans are black.

Just as propositional logic has a major rule (modus ponens) which reflects the basis of implication reasoning, predicate logic also has a major rule of inference, known as 'universal specialization'. The schema for this rule is shown below:

$$(\forall X) [f (X)], a \models f(a)$$

This states that if everything has the property f, and a is an individual (constant), then it can be inferred that a has the property f. Combining universal specialization and modus ponens, the following is also a valid schema:

$$(\forall X) [f (X) \rightarrow g (X)], f (a) \models g(a)$$

In this rule, a represents an individual constant. Thus the rule states that if generally, having the property f implies having the property g, and a is known to have the property f, then it can be concluded that a has the property g.

3.2.3 Semantics of predicate logic

The meaning of the propositional connectives was defined in terms of truth tables, i.e. as mappings from ordered pairs of the members of the set {T,F} to the set {T,F}. Similar truth-functional interpretations can be given for the wffs of predicate logic, although not quite so straightforwardly, since predicate names and individual constants and variables do not have truth values.

The basis of such an interpretation is a domain of individuals. Individual constants (or proper names – or in Prolog, the atoms used in a program) map directly on to members of this set, and individual variables range over them. In this scheme of interpretation, a one-place (or monadic) predicate denotes the set of individuals for which the predicate is true. The semantic **model** for predicate logic is concerned only with this **extensional** aspect of meaning. The extensional meaning of the predicate "dog(   )" is that subset of the domain of individuals which are dogs. The **intensional** meaning, which deals with the abstract concept of dogginess, is not represented in the model.

N-place predicates are treated similarly, as denoting ordered n-tuples from the domain of individuals for which the predicate is true. Building on these, precise meanings of the quantifiers can similarly be specified. A universally quantified formula, i.e. one having the form (∀X) F, where F contains X, is true if and only if every instance of F having an individual constant uniformly substituted for X is true. An existentially quantified formula is true if at least one substitution instance is true.

The purpose of this semantic analysis is not to show directly how real world situations can be represented in logic but rather to verify the formal properties of predicate logic. When we use such a logical notation to encode real-world knowledge, we take these formal properties for granted.

3.2.4 Logical inference

In the foregoing sections, some logical rules of inference have been introduced in passing, in a schematic form. In constructing a proof, there are several different logical rules from which to select. A human-oriented approach to theorem proving, called 'natural deduction' is heuristic in nature, and requires insight to select those rules whose invocation will contribute to the desired conclusion.

A mechanical inference procedure for predicate logic uses an approach of first reducing the variety of different types of wff, and then reducing the number of rules of inference to one. The former is possible because of the interdefinability of the various logical connectives and quantifiers (for example, in the way that the Boolean connectives in a logic circuit can all be constructed from different configurations of **nand** elements). A mechanical sequence of transformations, concerned with eliminating explicit quantifiers, is applied to a logic formula to render it in a normalized clausal form. In the clausal form, proofs can be constructed by repeated application of a single rule of inference, known as the rule of resolution. The theory of resolution is due to Robinson (1965), and the step-by-step operation of the transformation of predicate logic formulae to clausal form is expounded in Clocksin and Mellish (1984), Chapter 10 and Appendix B.

3.3 PREDICATE LOGIC AS A KNOWLEDGE REPRESENTATION

Predicate logic would seem an ideal basis for knowledge representation – it has considerable expressive power for representing the structure of propositions and rules; it has a precise semantics and known formal properties; it has mechanical inference procedures. Why should any other scheme of knowledge representation be necessary or desirable? Basically there are four kinds of motivation for using some alternative:

1   A less expressive formalism is sufficient for the task and proves to be simpler to construct and more efficient in operation. For example, the clausal form of logic embodied in Prolog may be used directly.
2   The logic needs to be extended to encode phenomena not expressible in predicate logic, for example, reasoning with defaults.

3 Irrespective of (**1**) or (**2**), a representation language of equivalent power to the chosen logic may be preferred for its more efficient access mechanisms during the inference process.

4 A representation language may be more human oriented than a very abstract formalism if, for example, it uses a two-dimensional graphical notation in which relationships can be made explicit.

3.4 ALTERNATIVE KNOWLEDGE REPRESENTATIONS

Altogether we consider three different representations below: Prolog, semantic networks and frames. For each, we outline the nature of the representation (except in the case of Prolog, which we have already met) and then consider first its expressive power, then its associated inference mechanism and finally the practicalities of its use in an IKBS.

3.5 PROLOG

The major limitations of Prolog's representational power are its restrictions compared with predicate logic. These are:

1 The negation as failure convention. It is not possible to assert explicitly that a certain proposition is false and exploit this in a proof. It is also not possible to prevent Prolog from denying a proposition which may be true but isn't recorded in the database.

2 Disjunctions may not be asserted, nor may they be concluded in the head of a rule.

3 Since Prolog has no symbol for any quantifiers, and all variables are treated as universally quantified, it is not possible to assert propositions involving existentially quantified variables.

3.5.1 The Prolog inference mechanism

The way Prolog attempts to prove a goal is intelligible withot explicit reference to resolution theorem proving, but its relationship to the latter can establish the soundness of its proof procedure.

The basis of resolution is the idea of 'proof by contradiction' and the rule of inference whose form is:

$$A \rightarrow B, {\sim}B \models {\sim}A$$

and for which

$$A, {\sim}A \models \square$$

is a special case. "□" denotes a contradiction, usually referred to as 'the empty denial'. To construct a proof by resolution, the desired conclusion is denied, and 'resolved' against clauses from the database by repeated application of the resolution rule until (if the proof is successful) the empty denial is derived.

3.5.2 Prolog as a practical knowledge representation formalism for IKBS

One of the attractions of Prolog for knowledge representation is that it not only provides the clause and rule formalism and the theorem prover but is a practical programming language in its own right. However, because the rule formalism and theorem prover are built into the language, it is not possible to inspect or interrupt a proof for the purposes of the justification facilities outlined at the end of chapter 1, unless a higher-level interpreter is written which treats rules as data.

Where it is desired to embed the theorem-proving capabilities of Prolog in a procedural shell, we run up against the inadequacies of the language's control primitives.

3.6 SEMANTIC NETWORKS

In the brief history of artificial intelligence and cognitive psychology, many diagrams have been constructed and called 'semantic networks'. In psychological research, such diagrams have been used to build models of the structure of human memory that could account for its 'associative' nature

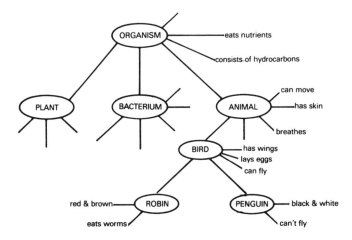

Fig. 3.1 Concept hierarchy as a semantic network

whereby speed of recall from long-term memory is correlated with the strength of meaning association between concepts. These studies concentrated on areas of knowledge where concepts are structured in a classification tree of sets and supersets, as shown in Fig. 3.1.

Beside showing how the set of things is classified and sub-classified, the diagram also shows how the **properties** of objects can be stored economically in a memory structure. Properties which are true of a whole class of objects need be stored only once in the network. Eating nutrients is a property of the class of organisms as a whole, and does not need to be repeated for any of its specific subclasses. The latter are assumed to **inherit** all properties of superclasses by default. To record attributes as economically as possible, even those, such as the ability to fly for birds, which are not true for all subclasses, are stored at the most general level. Exceptions such as penguins have an alternative value for the corresponding attribute. Such a contradictory value overrides the default.

Psychologists attempted to show experimentally that human memory is structured in this way. It was found that subjects could affirm or deny statements about the specific properties of objects quicker than those about properties that were true of very broad classes of things. They could also affirm or deny statements about class membership in proportion to the 'semantic distance' between the classes.

To serve as a general-purpose notation for knowledge and data, a network representation must represent individual objects and their class membership, and any situations or actions involving them. Figure 3.2 shows an example of such a network.

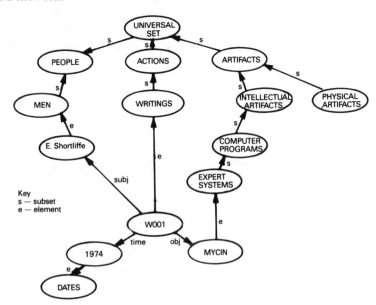

Fig. 3.2 Simple semantic network.

The example network expresses the proposition that E. Shortliffe wrote the MYCIN expert system in 1974, as well as providing further information about the classes of object that Shortliffe, MYCIN and 1974 are drawn from.

3.6.1 Structure of semantic nets

The basic building blocks of the network are nodes and arcs. Each arc connects exactly two nodes, is directed, and has a label. This is a restriction compared with logic clauses, in which we could have written much more concisely:

wrote (shortliffe, mycin, 1974)

On the other hand, in combination, these basic arcs can express extremely complex propositions, at the cost of having to create tokens with arbitrary entity names (such as W001 in Fig. 3.2) to encode relationships involving more than a pair of objects. To be consistent, arcs are never labelled with predicates that correspond to transitive verbs. The precise restrictions on what an arc may represent directly vary between instances of the semantic network representation. In some systems, arc labels are drawn from a small finite set including those for set relationships such as subset, disjoint subset and element, and symbols such as 'has' or 'has_part' to denote attributes.

In the logic clause, the role occupied by each argument is nowhere stated in the knowledge base, and has to be interpreted by a convention which is the responsibility of the builder of the knowledge base. The labelling of the arcs allows the role of each participant in an action to be made explicit, a feature that might be useful in generating explanations.

3.6.2 Logic and semantic networks

A number of variants on the semantic network notation were in use in the mid 1970's, in a range of different IKBS applications, including scene analysis, natural language question-answering and intelligent computer-aided instruction. The history of these is reviewed in Brachman (1979). These notations and the corresponding software were developed typically to solve the particular problem in hand, and did not allow the full expressive power that could be attained in predicate logic. Hendrix (1978), Deliyanni and Kowalski (1979) and others have investigated the logical status of network notations and have developed formalisms of power equivalent to that of predicate logic. Indeed, the semantic network is now viewed as an implementation framework for logic rather than as alternative to it. In Hendrix's notation, such logical operators as disjunction, implication and negation can be represented as subsets of the set of situations. The members of these sets are a special kind of node, a supernode, which partitions off a

space within a network. Figures 3.3 to 3.6 illustrate how spaces may be used to mark off those propositions that are not directly asserted from those that are.

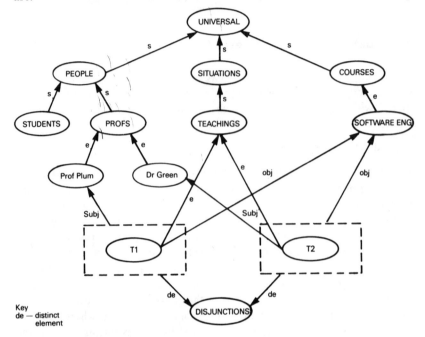

Fig. 3.3 Representation for 'Software Engineering is taught by Prof. Plum or Dr Green.'

The nodes labelled T1 and T2 both represent instances of the set of 'situations' or actions, but as they are not in the global space, neither is asserted as true. They may be thought of as invisible except when accessed via the link to the disjunctions set.

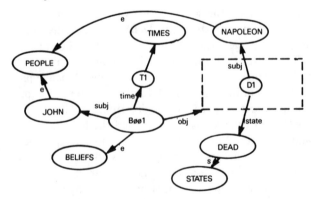

Fig. 3.4 Representation of 'John believes that Napoleon is dead'.

As with disjunctions, the reported beliefs of others are not asserted as true.

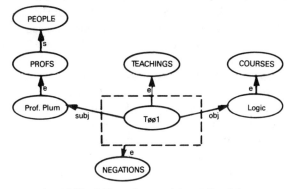

Fig. 3.5 Representation of 'Prof. Plum does not teach Logic'.

Again, we do not want negated propositions to be visible globally as though they were asserted to be true.

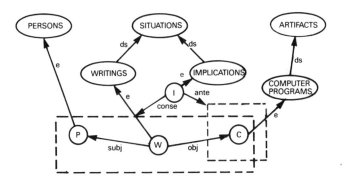

Fig. 3.6 Representation of 'If any computer program exists then somebody has written it'.

In Fig. 3.6, the basic framework for the representation of an implication is fairly obvious: an instance of an implication has an antecedent (ante) and a consequent link (con). However, the proposition in the example contains both an existentially quantified variable ('somebody' in English) and a universally quantified one (which stands for any computer program). We need to take a closer look at how individual constants and variables are represented.

An individual constant is a node which is in the global partition and which has one or more outgoing 'e' or 'de' arcs (but no 's' arcs). A variable is a node with a system-generated name which occurs within a partition.

Existential quantification is implicit wherever there is an assertion of a node within a space. Universal quantification of a node is indicated by its presence in both the antecedent and consequent space of an implication. It is in fact because arbitrary nesting of quantifiers (and the other forms of indirect assertion – negation, disjunction, belief) is possible that the concept of spaces or partitions is needed at all. (If nesting were not allowed then individual nodes could have been connected directly to the classes of disjunctions, implications, etc. as members.)

Querying a semantic network knowledge base is very like querying the Prolog database. The asserted propositions are all represented in a 'knowledge' space, and the goal or query has a separate space of its own. The deduction algorithm initially searches within the knowledge space for instantiations of the variables in the query within matching propositions. If nothing is asserted directly, then propositions that are 'buried' within logical expressions such as universally quantified implications are searched. Where necessary new subgoals are set up in a backward-chaining process.

The deduction process has to do the same work as a resolution theorem prover, but its implementation is more straightforward since the data structure is built out of simple uniform components. Search is also reduced by the availability of pointers linking all related objects and object classes.

Semantic networks in expert systems

There are two major uses for networks in an expert system: for representing objects and relationships, and for representing rules of inference in an inference network. The PROSPECTOR system used links in a network to represent the relationship between the conclusion and antecedents of each rule. The strength of association was represented by the labelling of the arc.

3.6.3 Evaluation of semantic networks

Semantic nets have a number of advantages: First, that of efficiency, gained by indexing the knowledge base on arguments as well as predicates. Deliyanni and Kowalski, however, argue that this feature can easily be incorporated into a logic theorem prover, to which the semantic network is otherwise equivalent. Secondly, the emphasis on the graphical notation and its object-oriented bias makes it more intelligible than a formal logic representation. Finally the extreme normalization of the knowledge structure into simple triples (arc and two nodes) forms the basis for a very straightforward concrete data structure, and this simplicity is being exploited in special machine architectures for parallel search of large knowledge bases.

A major disadvantage of semantic networks is that the object-orientation doesn't go far enough, because of the fragmentation of an object's properties into a multitude of arcs, and of the restriction on the labelling of arcs with predicate names.

3.7 FRAMES

One of the advantages of semantic networks is that while they are built out of very simple elements, the latter are clustered around nodes which correspond to significant objects in the world. In 'reading' a semantic network these objects may be regarded as units. This feature means that the network formalism provides a better tool of thought and medium of human communication than the direct use of predicate calculus notation. Taking this argument further, the use of larger building blocks for knowledge representation, known as **frames** has been proposed.

Like semantic nets, the idea of frames first arose as a metaphor for the organization of a memory or knowledge base before their structural characteristics were fully worked out. The concept was originally employed by Minsky to account for the recognition of objects in vision, but it quickly gained widespread popularity as a basis for knowledge representation in general.

The basic idea of a frame is rather like that of a record in data processing. All the attributes of an object are collected together in a single composite structure. Unlike the fields of a record in conventional programming, the frame's slots are labelled in each occurrence of the frame instead of being described in an external schema or declaration. An instance of a frame may lack a value for a given **slot**. (In fact, since the slot is labelled when present, it will lack the slot altogether.) To allow for the representation of multi-valued attributes, a slot may have a number of **facets**.

3.7.1 An early frame language: FRL

FRL (Frame Representation Language) is described in Roberts and Goldstein (1977) and also featured as a chapter in Winston and Horn (1980). An individual frame is a list structure, such as the following:

```
(IKBS
    (NAME    ($VALUE  (| Intelligent Knowledge-Based Systems|)))
    (AKO     ($VALUE  (Third-year-options Paper-3)))
    (TUTOR   ($VALUE  (Conroy)))
    (TIME    ($VALUE  (MON-11)))
    (PLACE   ($VALUE  (R11)))
)
```

The notation is that of LISP, in which FRL is written, where a list is made up of atoms and/or lists, and the elements are separated by spaces (rather than by commas, as in Prolog). In the example, the frame's name is the first element in the list, and the remainder of the frame is a number of slots, shown here one to a line. Each slot is named and has a filler which stores the value or values. Since a slot can have multiple values, the filler is a list. In the example, one of the slots, AKO, has two values, but the others all have one.

In FRL, frames are supported by creation and deletion functions, as well as those for selectively updating slots. In addition, frames provide for property inheritance, through the AKO ('A Kind Of') slot, whose values are links to other frames, rather like the element and subset links in a semantic network.

A frame is, however, more than a passive data structure. Procedures can be attached to slots; for example, an 'If Needed' procedure attached to a particular slot will be invoked automatically if a value for the slot is required and none is explicitly stored. The procedure can be an arbitrary LISP function. Actions can also be taken whenever a slot is updated, if it has an 'If Added' or 'If Removed' slots.

3.7.2 Frames and prototypes

As with the nodes in a semantic network, a frame can be used to represent either a class or an individual object. In a class frame, we might want to store both properties of the class and default properties of the members, but these should not be confused. In the semantic network the distinction is made clear by the use of distinct labels for member and subset links, but in FRL there is only one kind of inheritance link.

More recent frame languages such as KEE (Fikes and Kehler, 1985) as well as applications developed using frames (cf. Aikins, 1983), have emphasized the use of frames to store **prototype** descriptions of objects. In KEE, those properties which are true of an object or class itself are described in 'own slots', whereas those which comprise a prototypical description of members or instances are described in 'member slots'. Slots of either type have a number of facets besides the value, which specify constraints on the latter. These include the value class, maximum and minimum cardinality, units, comments to be used in interaction with the user.

The value class specification and the cardinality limits are particularly important, since they allow the frame language the ability to represent quantified assertions and to make appropriate inferences.

3.7.3 Integrating frames and rules

In an IKBS built using frames, the ability to embed procedural code within the knowledge structure removes the need to have a general purpose inference mechanism such as a resolution theorem prover. This, however, would seem to go against the grain of knowledge-based systems which seek to separate knowledge and control as much as possible. One motivation for doing so is to avoid the restrictions on control strategy that a simple production system imposes. Within a frame system, it is much easier to provide a control regime that matches that of a domain expert, or can be modified in the light of user feedback. To retain the desirable characteristics of modularity and declarativeness in a frame-structured knowledge base, the arbitrary LISP coded procedures can be constrained to production rule format. Production rules can themselves be represented as frames with the principal slots being antecedents and consequents.

Aikins (1983) re-implemented the PUFF system for diagnosis and management of respiratory diseases using a frame architecture. In this system, named CENTAUR, each possible diagnostic category – both disease types and degrees of severity – was represented as a prototype frame. In such a frame, permissible value ranges for the attributes which constituted the evidence factors for the disease are stored as facets of the 'components' slot. Disease prototype frames also had slots for actions to be carried out if the hypothesis is confirmed, and slots for production rules, which are classified into a number of distinct groups according to their role in the consultation. For example, summary rules select texts to include in the output produced at the end of a consultation, and triggering rules select disease prototypes for further investigation on the basis of symptoms or other conclusions already reached.

In addition to domain knowledge frames, there are also control frames, which specify the consultation strategy. It is even possible for the user to select a strategy from a choice of three: confirmation (try the prototype which best matches the data first), elimination (worst match first), and fixed order. This allowed the system to explicitly represent control information, instead of having it implicit, for example in the order of premises in rules. Explicit control strategies, where a consultation takes place in a series of logically distinct stages which are meaningful to the expert and user, is possible to a much greater extent than in a pure production system. The modularity of knowledge in a frame system is at a much higher level than in a production system, and this feature enables the knowledge base as a whole to be more intelligible, and easier to modify.

3.7.4 Evaluation of frames

The major advantages of frames lie in the ability to represent structured data objects and relationships, augmented by procedures for default and inheritance reasoning. Procedural attachment makes it possible to link the specification of actions to that of objects, removing much of the need for general inference procedures. Most applications using frames have used them to complement other forms of knowledge representation, particularly production rules, rather than to supplant them.

SUMMARY
Chapter 3

Non-trivial expert systems need a sophisticated represent-ation of knowledge in terms of objects and relationships as well as conditions and actions.

Logic forms a basis for representing knowledge and provides a standard by which other notations can be compared.

Propositional logic specifies the valid inferences that can be made from a given proposition. An important rule of inference, called 'modus ponens' models the inference process at the heart of expert systems.

Propositional logic lacks generality, since it does not represent the internal structure of propositions. Predicate logic uses variables and quantifiers to represent truths about classes of individuals.

Mechanical inference procedures, based on the 'resolu-tion' principle, exist for propositional and predicate logic in a normalized clausal form. Prolog is a subset of predicate logic in clausal form for which the inference procedure is efficient.

The simplifications in Prolog in comparison with predicate logic mean that its expressive power is limited. In particular, the language does not support directly the assertion of negations, disjunctions or existentially quantified formulae.

Alternative knowledge representations include graphical notations known as 'semantic networks' and 'frames' These find favour because the arguments to a proposition can be labelled, and because inferences about the properties an object inherits from classes and superclasses it belongs to can be made efficiently.

Semantic networks can be made expressively equivalent to predicate logic by notational devices such as 'partitioning'. However, they do need to be supported by inference procedures which are logically sound.

Frames are similar to networks, but represent structured objects directly rather than as the composition of several binary predicates.

EXERCISES
Chapter 3

E3.1 Decide on a representation in Prolog for the tree shown in Fig. 3.1. Develop a program that will tell you if an individual class of organism has a given property (which may of course be inherited from one of its superclasses). A program to do something similar is listed in Coelho *et al.* (1982). Modify the program so that it can also tell all the organisms that have a given property.

E3.2 Develop a Prolog knowledge base that will record all the facts shown in Fig. 3.2, not just the event W001.

E3.3 Draw a semantic network to represent the proposition: 'John said that anyone who takes Artificial intelligence is either foolish or brilliant'.

E3.4 Using a book such as the 'Family Medical Adviser', encode the information given about a number of diseases in a frame notation. Try to rewrite it in production rule form.

4

DEVELOPING EXPERT SYSTEMS: 'KNOWLEDGE ENGINEERING'

In this chapter, we look at the development life-cycle of expert systems, and then examine techniques for the significant phases. We start at the point where the appropriateness and feasibility of an expert system for a problem are assessed. 'Knowledge Engineering' with and without machine assistance is considered next, and finally, the main alternative implementation strategies and software tools are examined.

4.1 THE EXPERT SYSTEM DEVELOPMENT LIFE-CYCLE

Conventional computer system development is considered to take place sequentially with phases for feasibility study, requirements investigation and analysis, specification, design, implementation, testing, integration testing, deployment and maintenance. This approach is classically found to its full extent in information systems (data processing). System software projects and real-time systems place less emphasis on the stages before specification, but this is largely because end-users are less involved and processing logic is more important than the form and content of input and output. Nevertheless, all stages are logically required even if not perceived as distinct by a programmer.

We have noted in Chapter 1 that although there are some non-interactive (or embedded) expert systems, interactive advisory programs are more common. As such, expert systems are crucially dependent for their successful acceptance on the extent to which they engage in a meaningful dialogue with the user. To do this, emphasis must be given to the way the knowledge is represented and presented by the system. Accordingly, the traditional life-cycle model, with its emphasis on the pre-implementation stages of investigation, analysis, specification and design, describes satisfactorily what must take place in an expert system project.

However, there is a trend in all computer application areas to look for ways of cutting down the effort needed to develop an application and hence its cost. A serious problem is that of communication between the developer and users or expert informants in requirements investigation. This problem is exacerbated by the long gap between the specification being fixed on paper and the emergence of its working realization. Written specifications may not be clear to users, who are forced to take on trust that the designers have faithfully translated their requirements. They do not have an opportunity to verify the specification until the working system is delivered. This problem is even more severe with expert systems, where neither the potential users nor the expert informant may have any idea what to expect. As an interactive system, it is also difficult to specify using current approaches.

One solution to these problems that is being increasingly advocated and adopted is the use of high-level tools whose primitives closely match the concepts of the domain. If such highly productive tools are available, then an approach of prototyping becomes feasible. A rapidly developed prototype can be used to bring life to the discussions between the developer and expert or user who can provide timely feedback to the development process.

Prototyping runs counter to the prevailing software engineering philosophy, which is to delay implementation until the design is fully worked out. The rationale for this is to improve the correctness of programs. However, most software failures result from faulty specification rather than faulty coding. Prototypes help to make the full implications of the specification and design explicit as early as possible. Most expert systems that have been introduced into industrial or commercial settings have been developed using a prototyping approach, where an initial version has been developed quickly and then steadily refined. It is feasible to take this approach only if appropriate high-level tools exist. The first industrially applied systems were developed by research laboratories that had already identified what facilities an expert system generating tool (or 'shell') should provide. Now the prototyping approach can be followed using commercial products, some derived from the research tools, but more commonly specially written by software houses.

4.2 FEASIBILITY AND APPROPRIATENESS

It has been noted already that most expert systems are interactive and also that many proposals for the creation of an expert system are made in the absence of a clear understanding of what expert systems are. This will be true particularly if the initiative for the development comes from the intended user rather than from the developer. For both reasons the activities associated with the early phases of software development will require extra emphasis. The first stage is to decide whether an expert system is an appropriate solution to the problem. The fashionable novelty of the subject leads many people to claim that they need an expert system when what they mean is an interactive computer program.

The first task in a proposed expert system project is to evaluate the problem. Is it a task for which an expert system is an appropriate response?

To do this, it is necessary to have a clear idea of what an expert system is – Chapter 1 should have helped – and also what it is not. As a reminder of what an expert system is, we can use a checklist to which we expect more than one affirmative answer:

1 Does the application have the functional characteristics of expert systems? Does it involve providing advice on problem cases from within a well-defined area of expert knowledge?
2 Is there uncertainty in the knowledge of the problem domain?
3 Should the program be expected to accept uncertain input from the user and still come up with (qualified) advice?
4 Is the problem area an important one where the user's confidence in the program's conclusions is an issue? Is justification of the line of reasoning required?
5 Most importantly, is an expert on the application available?

Even if a majority of these questions are answered affirmatively, it is important to consider whether there is not an alternative and more straightforward approach to implementation. Perhaps the problem has been misclassified as an expert system application, when some other kind of computer program might be more appropriate. The examples in Chapter 1 of applications not considered to be expert systems illustrate this possibility. From now on in this chapter, however, we will assume that an expert system is to be developed.

4.3 KNOWLEDGE ELICITATION

Having delimited the problem and identified it as an expert system task, the first step is to obtain a source of expert knowledge. In any significant area of application this will mean a human expert, rather than a written source. The effectiveness of a system is limited by the quality of knowledge encoded in it, so it is not possible to construct a system giving expert-level performance using knowledge supplied by inexpert informants.

With the expert, the phase of investigation or knowledge elicitation may begin. It is assumed that the expert is not part of the project development team, and has no prior knowledge of the techniques of expert systems. There is therefore a role for a member of the project team to perform the role which a systems analyst does in information system development. The person who is responsible for eliciting knowledge for an expert system has been termed a 'knowledge engineer'.

4.3.1 Characteristics of expert knowledge

If an expert can say precisely how the expertise is applied to any problem, he or she has described an algorithm. Since a computer program for automating such expertise can be designed directly from the algorithm, no special techniques are needed.

Expert system techniques are for problems whose solution cannot easily be described in that way. Typical experts in medicine, geology, design or fault finding do not seem able to describe algorithms that are guaranteed to work on any problem they may face. We may sum up this phenomenon by saying that experts do not know what they know. They may be able to articulate textbook knowledge about the underlying scientific principles of their discipline, but not general rules for the application to problem instances.

Problems of a diagnostic nature are approached typically by pattern matching, where sets of observable symptoms are associated with hypothesized underlying causes. The relationship between symptoms and diseases or faults in general is one for which there ought to exist some causal mechanism. However, sometimes such causal explanations are not known in full detail, as they are still the subject of basic scientific investigation. Even where there is a complete scientific model of the underlying process, the expert does not need to apply the model process each time a diagnosis is required. The association between cause and consequence may be said to be 'compiled' in the expert's mind.

Such knowledge is learned from experience but, because it has been learned inductively in this way, it may be wrong, or insufficiently discriminating, and is referred to as 'heuristic' or 'judgemental' knowledge.

4.3.2 How to elicit knowledge

It follows from these remarks about expert knowledge that a knowledge engineer is not going to get far with very open-ended questions such as 'how do you diagnose diseases in wheat?'. It is also inappropriate to place much reliance on textbook knowledge, although such sources may be appropriate for basic familiarization about the problem.

The knowledge engineer must elicit knowledge in smaller units. We have stated already that the judgemental knowledge of an expert often takes the form of associations between hypothesized causes and observable evidence for them. The production rule, introduced in Chapter 1 is a suitable notation for encoding such associations. At the initial stages of elicitation, it is appropriate to write down the conditions and conclusions or actions in English. However, at a later stage, it is going to be necessary to consider the structure within the conditions and conclusions further, ultimately choosing a representation formalism in which knowledge can be represented in the computer system. For elicitation, however, a 'structured English' notation for production rules should be used, partly because it is intelligible to the expert informant as well as the developer.

These individual chunks of knowledge are small, as well as being relatively inaccessible, so the knowledge engineer is faced with a problem of devising a strategy for eliciting them. We have noted that expert problem solving knowledge is organized for application to specific problems, so it seems sensible to approach elicitation through sample problem cases. The 'method' for eliciting rules is therefore to ask the expert informant to justify his or her conclusions for each of a sample set of problem cases. Each time a justification is given such as

I concluded A because B, C and D but not E

the knowledge engineer has the basis of a rule for inclusion in the knowledge base. In the dialogue, the knowledge engineer will seek to elicit the expert's view of the relative importance of each of the reasons (conditions) and how they in turn can be established, and the strength of his belief in the conclusion.

4.3.3 Prototype development

Within the conventional computer system life-cycle model, all elicitation of knowledge would take place before any of it is encoded and the system is implemented and tested. In the prototyping approach, a small knowledge base can be developed on the computer quickly and tried out in practice. It would be usual first to test it against the cases used in the previous elicitation phase. If the computer's conclusions differ from those of the expert for these cases, then either the rules deduced by the knowledge engineer from the expert's explanations were defective, or else something has gone wrong in translating them into an internal form for the computer.

In either case, the solution is to attempt to rectify the rules. This can be done using the facilities provided in the inference engine for 'justifying' its conclusions. Exercising this option after each erroneous conclusion, the faulty rules can be identified and refined.

Once the original test cases are concluded satisfactorily, the knowledge base can be assessed against new test cases. Where the rules lack either sufficient generality or sufficient discrimination for these new cases, they can either be modified or new rules added to the knowledge base.

The feedback cycle in the prototype refinement approach may be summarized as:

1 Select new set of test cases.
2 Elicit rules or rule refinements from expert to account for new problem cases.
3 Encode new rules in the language of the selected software.
4 Test new knowledge base against current problem set with the expert as critic.
5 Repair rules until they work for current problem set.

At the end of any of these cycles, the knowledge base should be in a consistent state where it has been 'black box tested' against a set of problem cases. It can never be said to be complete. New test cases may not be handled correctly without modifying or adding to the knowledge base.

To put it bluntly, software developed in this way cannot be trusted. The best that can be hoped for is that the proportion of cases handled correctly is very much higher than that of those handled in error. The error rate that can be tolerated will vary according to the problem area, the error rate of human experts, and the importance attached to the conclusions. During the development process, the error rate in tests with new problem cases should be monitored, and should be seen to reduce over time. The system can be put into routine use if and when its performance exceeds that agreed as acceptable, but results should still be logged in order to provide feedback on the ongoing activity of knowledge refinement.

4.3.4 Encoding knowledge

In our discussion of the prototype refinement cycle for an expert system we have made scant reference to the process of translating the rules contributed by the expert informant into a formalism suitable for the computer. In the preliminary elicitation phase, representing the conditions and conclusions in unanalysed English was encouraged. The simplest mapping of rules like this into a formalism is to treat each condition and each conclusion as a proposition not to be analysed further. This indeed will be the only formalism supported by many of the expert system software 'shells'. (We discuss the characteristics of these in the last major section of this chapter.)

As we saw in the chapter on knowledge representation and inference, whether this is satisfactory depends on an analysis of the types of entity in the problem domain and their occurrences. Briefly, a propositional formalism is adequate if no entity type in the universe of discourse has more than one occurrence for which attribute values are needed in rule conditions in a single invocation of the knowledge base.

As an illustration of this, consider the PROSPECTOR and MYCIN systems. In the former, many different entities have different values for an attribute such as texture. However in the context of a single consultation with the software only one occurrence is understood, viz. the rocks in the visible landscape. 'The rocks have a porphyritic texture' can therefore be treated as an unanalysed proposition (which has the advantage that it can be queried or asserted to the user directly from the text). However, if the application required the values of the same attributes for several different geological strata, a more elaborate formalism would be necessary.

In MYCIN, the top-level goal is to determine a single REGIMEN or treatment for infections each comprising more than one organism. To do this, it is necessary first to identify each of the organisms. The identity of an organism is an attribute that will occur once for each occurrence of an organism in the infection. Similarly, the observable attributes used to establish the identity of the organisms will each occur several times per consultation. It is not possible in advance to know how many distinct organisms will be found in a given patient's cultures, and it is anyway not reasonable to build such redundancy into rules as illustrated below:

If the morphology of the first organism is rod, . . .

If the morphology of the second organism is rod, . . .

If the morphology of the third organism is rod, . . .

The correct representation for such knowledge is general rules with variable slots for entity occurrences, e.g.

If the morphology of <organism> is rod, . . .

In MYCIN, entities like organism that may occur more than once are marked as such in the knowledge base, and the control mechanism is able to apply correctly the same generic rule once for each occurrence. Rules that reference the attributes of such entities must state explicitly how the multiple values are to be combined (a different task from combining certainties).

Also in the MYCIN domain, there are hierarchical relationships: organisms can occur multiply in cultures, which themselves occur multiply for each patient. In a consultation, the system has to establish how many instances of such entities exist in the given case, before enquiring about the attributes of each instance. To help manage this aspect of the working database, MYCIN makes use of an explicit data model, the 'context tree', to show the generic relationships between entities in its universe of discourse.

4.4 ANALYSIS AND DESIGN OF KNOWLEDGE BASES

If it is possible to be satisfied at the outset that a propositional logic-based system will suffice for an application, then an expert system can be built using the iterative prototyping approach outlined above, without any further concern for design methods. It will be possible to map the elicited knowledge easily on to the language of a simple proprietary expert system shell package, and refine the knowledge-base using the justification facilities provided. In simple applications, the constraints of the knowledge representation language will serve to focus the dialogue between the developer and expert, particularly when uncertainty in rules is to be modelled.

If on the other hand, there are complex relationships between entities in the domain of discourse that need to be built into the knowledge base, a conceptual analysis is needed.

One way to do this is to analyse the propositions in the conditions and conclusions of rules and express their structure using predicate calculus. Rules framed in this way may have quantified predicates in either conditions or actions. It may be necessary to extend the logic to deal with degrees of certainty.

An alternative approach is to adapt methods of conceptual modelling developed for the analysis of more conventional computer systems. Addis (1985) makes a case for approaching the design of knowledge-based systems through 'Extended Relational Analysis'. This form of analysis can be used as the basis for structuring the data in the working database of a production system just as it is used in the design of organizational databases.

4.4.1 Normalization

The first step is to 'normalize' an initial data model. We will illustrate the technique with some 'labdata' such as MYCIN uses. (The example is fictitious, so it may not make sense to a reader with medical knowledge):

patient_id	sex	age	culture_id	date	org_id	morph	stain	i
p1234	f	45	c5678	9/11	1	rod	neg	?
p1234	f	45	c5678	9/11	2	coc	pos	?
p1234	f	45	c5791	22/11	1	coc	pos	?
p1357	m	63	c5884	22/11	1	coc	pos	?
p1357	m	63	c5884	22/11	2	coc	neg	?

Fig. 4.1   Unnormalized lab data used in a MYCIN-like system.

Figure 4.1 shows sample lab data laid out in a tabular form. We can imagine that the laboratory analysts record their findings on such a form, with the information in the patient_id, culture_id and date columns identifying the source of the cultures and that in the right three columns describing the individual organisms found there.

Normalization is concerned with removing redundancy in the underlying data model. One type of redundancy occurs where groups of data occurrences (rows in the table) share the same identifying attributes. There are two such repeating groups in the data model shown: the culture data (culture_id and those attributes to its right) and the individual organism data (org_id and attributes to its right). The normalization method sees such repeating groups as entities in their own right and they are removed from the original entity and a key or set of identifying attributes established. In the present case, after two applications of the repeating group rule, we get separate entity types with table headings as shown:

PATIENT

patient_id	sex	age

CULTURE

culture_id	patient_id	date

ORGANISM

culture_id	organism_id	morph	stain	id

The identifying attributes in each case are shown underlined. Note that when a repeating group is removed from a 'parent' entity, the identifier of the parent must be included among the new entity's attributes. (This ensures that the relationship between the two entities is recorded.) Where a parent identifier is copied into the attributes of a repeating group, it may become part of a compound identifier for that entity, depending on whether there is another attribute or attribute set that can uniquely identify the entity. There are further rules for removing redundant information, but the data model in our example is fully normalized already. The test is whether 'every determinant is a candidate key'. A determinant is an attribute or set of attributes that functionally determines another attribute. This in turn means that given a value for the former, the value of the latter is determined. This relationship between identifiers and each of the other attributes can be seen to hold in the normalized tables shown.

Removing redundancy can have the obvious benefit of saving memory space, but that is not the motivation for the technique. The real reason is that it ensures the integrity of the database, given some constraints on updates, such as not permitting identifying attributes to be changed.

An additional benefit of normalization is that it suggests a uniform way of representing entities. If we were using Prolog for the working database of an expert system, it would be possible to represent each tuple (or entity instance) as a simple assertion, in a form such as:

culture (Culture_id, Patient_id, Date).

Having separated attributes into separate entities, it is possible always to trace relationships between them, where one entity has the identifier of another as one of its attributes. In our example, the relationship between patient and culture is implicit through the shared attribute patient_id, and that between culture and organism through culture_id.

4.4.2 Entity-relationship analysis

A normalized data model is one in which separate entities have been described and identified, and in which it is possible to infer relationships by the sharing of attributes. Further analysis can be carried out into the qualities of the relationships. Whether a relationship is one to many can usually be predicted by reference to the shared attribute that marks it: A relationship marked by a key in entity A and a non-key or part-key in entity B is normally a one to many relationship from A to B. Other features of relationships that can have a bearing on database integrity include:

- whether relationships are optional or obligatory on all occurrences of the related entity types, i.e. whether entity occurrences can exist in the database without being related to other entities.
- whether relationships are related to each other (for example, is one relationship a subset of another?, or are two relationships mutually exclusive?).

There are many variant notations for recording such an analysis, of which that described in Addis (1985) is one. Others can be found in most recent textbooks on databases and systems analysis. At the design stage of the development of an expert system, the importance of a conceptual data analysis is to determine if there are any to-many relationships between entities. In such cases, it will be necessary to use a knowledge representation scheme more sophisticated than a propositional logic for the working database. Normalized entity models map directly on to clausal logic, and entity relationship models show how a semantic network scheme can be employed. This latter approach is compatible with the way knowledge is represented in EMYCIN. ('EMYCIN' – Empty MYCIN – is the name given to an expert system shell derived from the original MYCIN software and made domain-independent so that new knowledge bases can be developed using the same inference engine.)

4.5 CHOICE OF CONTROL STRATEGY

While diagnostic consultation systems appear to be the most typical, there are other classes of problem for which expert systems have been developed. There are also general characteristics of the knowledge and data sources such as size and reliability that differentiate applications. Both of these factors influence the choice of a control strategy.

In Chapter 1, we introduced two main alternative strategies for the control mechanism of an expert system, backward and forward chaining. Other important attributes of the control mechanism are:

- whether it is deterministic or nondeterministic (the Prolog proof procedure illustrates the latter with its backtracking mechanism),
- whether it deals with uncertain knowledge or data (and how),
- whether (and how) rules are selected to eliminate the firing of those unlikely to influence the solution.
- whether the knowledge base includes meta-rules designed to influence the control strategy (to enable the system's reasoning to more closely resemble that of human experts).
- how it assimilates data and knowledge from multiple sources (for example by using a concurrent processing strategy instead of a sequential inference technique).

Hayes-Roth, Waterman and Lenat (1983) and Alty and Coombs (1984) both discuss these alternatives and their use in various example systems from the research literature.

4.5.1 Automating the knowledge engineering process

Robert Kowalski has been quoted in the computing press as predicting that knowledge engineering will be the shortest-lived profession ever. His justification for this remark is that the skills practised by a knowledge engineer are just as suitable for augmenting by an expert system as any other professional expertise. A number of systems have been developed in research laboratories which aim to provide automated aids for the knowledge engineer.

Perhaps the best known of these systems is TEIRESIAS, (Davis and Lenat, 1982). The goal of this system is to enable a domain expert to refine a knowledge base without the aid of a knowledge engineer. It is assumed that a prototype rule base exists already, and is to be refined by a process of testing against case data and the amendment or addition of rules to cover for new cases, as discussed above.

The help that TEIRESIAS provides is in pinning down the precise source of error when a wrong conclusion is reached. The program guides the user through the use of the justification tracing mechanism starting from its conclusions. It is based on the MYCIN expert system architecture. The user is asked by TEIRESIAS whether any conclusions have been missed or if any of those given should not have been drawn.

For a conclusion made in error, the program finds the rules that were fired to reach that conclusion and asks the user to identify which condition should not have been satisfied or to provide additional conditions. For a conclusion omitted, TEIRESIAS starts by locating rules which can make the desired conclusion and shows which conditions in them failed. Both kinds of error can involve tracing backwards to antecedent rules. If neither strategy for repairing existing rules works, then a new rule is needed, and TEIRESIAS can help in identifying when this is necessary and what its conclusion should be.

Automating the rule refinement process does not cover the entire process of knowledge engineering. In particular, since it operates on a defective but existing set of rules, it does not address the problem of how to start the analysis and design. Bennett (1985) describes ROGET, a system for determining the overall conceptual structure of an expert system which can be used to start developing a new system from scratch.

The basis of the ROGET approach is that expert systems can be classified according to the tasks they address and their internal structuring of major subgoals. For example, MYCIN's main goal is to determine the antibiotics to prescribe for a patient, in turn requiring that the organisms to treat, microbiological cultures, clinical signs, history, surgeries and burns are identified. It can be seen as a specific instance of a class of expert systems whose main goal is to determine a set of *recommended actions*. This class of systems in turn requires *determined causes, laboratory test results, observed signs* and *predisposing factors* to be identified. *Organisms to treat* is a narrower descriptor than *determined causes*, and *clinical signs, clinical history* and *surgeries* are similarly narrower terms than *observed signs, predisposing factors* and *important events* respectively. It is this thesaural arrangement of classes and instances of expert systems and their components that is the basis for the name 'ROGET'.

In a dialogue with ROGET, the user is first asked if the envisaged system resembles a known existing system. If it does, then the structural correspondences between the two systems are established. If it does not resemble an existing system known to both ROGET and the user, the dialogue proceeds to establish a higher-level description which can later be refined. From a refined description prototype rules can then be developed in the language of the particular expert system building tool that is to be used to build the performance program.

XPLAIN (Swartout 1983) is a further system in the research literature that seeks to help the process of developing an expert system. A major concern in this program is that the generated expert system should have good explanation facilities. The XPLAIN architecture partitions domain knowledge into two components, a *domain model* that represents the causal relationships in the application domain, and *domain principles* which are metarules or high-level generalizations of the structure of rules in the system. A typical domain principle comprises a goal, a domain rationale written in terms of the concepts in the domain model and a prototype method.

XPLAIN has another component, the *writer*, that uses the domain knowledge and domain principles to generate automatically the performance program. The latter is able to produce explanations that relate current goals to the underlying causal model of the domain and an *English generator* weaves these into a smooth dialogue.

4.6 SOFTWARE FOR EXPERT SYSTEMS

An expert system should meet the following general requirements irrespective of the application:

1 It should represent adequately the knowledge of the chosen problem domain.
2 It should apply the knowledge in a reasoning strategy that is both efficient and intelligible to the user.
3 It should have a good human interface if it is to overcome natural resistance to innovation and to remain in day to day use.
4 It should integrate where possible with existing sources of information and other software, so as not to ask the user questions that might be considered superfluous.

The first two requirements have been discussed above. The latter two requirements will be considered now, before reviewing the software alternatives and the criteria for their selection.

4.6.1 The human interface

There are two different roles in which people other than the knowledge engineer interact with an expert system, and both need consideration in the 'human engineering' of a system:

1 As an expert contributing the contents of the knowledge base. It is normally considered that the expert need not interact directly with the software, but through a dialogue with the knowledge engineer. However, in the evaluation and refinement of a prototype system, the expert will require feedback on the form and contents of the knowledge base. For the expert, the important human interface is the representation of knowledge in the system, and the extent to which it matches his own perception of the structure of his expert knowledge. The justification and debugging tools of the system will be used extensively in knowledge-base refinement and testing, and so they too should have an intelligible human interface.

2   As a user. A new user will expect firstly that adequate help is offered both at the beginning of the dialogue and at any point when input is solicited. Three forms of help should be provided in addition to the tracing or justification facilities that distinguish expert systems: First, help on the system options the user may exercise in the course of the dialogue. Second, help on selecting a hypothesis for the system to test (especially where the reasoning strategy is backward chaining). Third, amplification on the meaning of a particular question in the form of associated help text.

It should also be possible in implementing an effective human interface to insert arbitrary text into the knowledge base to be displayed as commentary on the intermediate or final conclusions reached by the system. This is made possible by allowing the output of advisory text to be one of the actions in the conclusion part of a rule.

For justification and explanation of the line of reasoning to be successful, it is desirable that the reasoning strategy employed matches closely that of the human expert. Expert system shell software packages differ in the extent to which they allow the knowledge engineer to exercise such control.

All users will expect questions to be phrased in a natural manner, and not to be redundant. For example, if the answers to a number of questions form a mutually exclusive set, they should be presented together as a choice.

4.6.2   Integration with other data and software

There are several circumstances in which it is desirable not to build an expert system as a self-contained application.

First, if the conditions reference data that is already available on the computer, especially if the user knows that it is on file. One reason that MYCIN is not in routine use is that it does not have access to medical records. Each consultation requires all the information to be entered by the user, although the basic patient data and details of previous investigations can reasonably be expected to be available in a database. Having to provide such data redundantly is a source of irritation that will lead to serious user resistance to expert systems. To make an expert system attractive to users, it has to be invoked with as little effort as possible, and ideally it should be fully integrated with operational programs and databases. This implies a design decision about allocating functions between the expert system and the external database.

4.6.3 Shells and AI languages

There are two principal software alternatives for developing expert systems: an expert system 'shell' software package, and a more general-purpose programming language.

Shells are so called because they are empty of any specific domain knowledge. Many of them have been developed out of the software used to develop a specific application in the past, although others have been developed specifically as generic tools.

Expert systems are now a sufficiently popular potential application area that there are scores of shells on the market, so the developer has a difficult job evaluating them and selecting one for a given application.

The products are differentiated by the problems they address. The majority address the provision of 'performance programs' by concentrating on the run-time capabilities, whereas others address the problems of knowledge-base development and refinement. We discuss techniques of machine learning and their application to knowledge acquisition in the next chapter, so for the remainder of the present chapter we concentrate on software of the former type.

Within this class of software, individual products vary according to the power of the knowledge representation formalism they support, the inference strategies employed (and whether a choice or a mixture of strategies can be used), their human factoring, their external interfaces, as well as such pragmatic considerations as knowledge-base size and performance limitations, machine availability and lastly, cost.

Perhaps the most important of the considerations is the knowledge representation supported. The major distinction is between those that are production-rule oriented and those that are object-oriented. The latter term is intended to embrace both network and frame representations. Pure production rule systems typically provide a formalism that is more limited than predicate logic, whereas object-oriented systems generally have more expressive power. Unfortunately systems of the latter sort (for example KEE, see Chapter 5), are at the time of writing available only on expensive high-performance workstations, whereas many alternative production rule systems are available for personal computers.

The typical expert system shell is marketed as a package of two components, a compiler to translate the rule-base, expressed in a language peculiar to the package, into an internal representation, and a run-time system to apply the compiled knowledge base in a consultation with the user. Sometimes an interactive knowledge-base structure editor is provided.

Shell packages are the most straightforward means of rapidly prototyping an expert system, with the developer having nothing at all to contribute to providing the inference strategy and run-time support. Run-time facilities usually include the following:

- Amplification of the meaning of a question. (The text for this has to have been inserted into the knowledge base by the developer.)
- Provision for the user to change previous answers to a question and have the impact of the new answer propagated through the previously derived conclusions.
- Provision for the user to volunteer answers to questions before they are asked. Normally this is implemented by the user typing an option letter and then having a numbered list of questions presented for selection. In the future, systems with a natural language interface will enable such a 'mixed initiative' dialogue to take place more naturally.
- Inspection of the working database, to allow the user to see the answers previously given and derived values for other goals.
- Justification. This may be provided 'on demand', where the user effectively asks, 'Why am I being asked this question?'. On-demand justification usually operates recursively so that the complete line of reasoning can be traced. Alternatively, some shells provide a post-consultation trace of the line of reasoning.

4.6.4 Artificial intelligence programming languages

One of the major limitations of many shells is the lack of a powerful representation formalism. Many of them are equivalent to programming languages supporting only simple Boolean and numeric variables. For this reason, it may be desirable to consider using one of the programming languages associated with artificial intelligence, namely Prolog, reviewed in Chapter 2, and LISP.

These languages lack the run-time components of an expert system. Prolog has a built-in inference mechanism but if the rules of the knowledge base are encoded in 'raw' Prolog, they are not available for inspection by the various run-time facilities. It is necessary, therefore to build a rule-interpreter and to code the rules as data. This means that Prolog (and LISP) are not as suitable for prototyping as an off-the-shelf shell. However, their powerful data structures, built-in search mechanisms and interpretive nature makes them a better building tool than conventional Pascal-like languages.

**SUMMARY
Chapter 4**

Developing an expert system is much like developing any other type of computer program. Implementation must be preceded by assessment of feasibility, and the analysis of requirements, although these are likely to change during the life of the project.

A prototyping approach is most commonly used. This

allows the knowledge base to be refined in response to feedback and evaluation. It is also made possible by software that provides helpful tracing output.

The process of obtaining the detailed contents of the knowledge base from the expert is referred to as 'knowledge elicitation'. This is not easy, since experts find it difficult to articulate their own knowledge.

As the knowledge base is designed for use in solving individual problems, the best way to build it is to base knowledge elicitation around test cases. The expert is asked for his conclusions on each case, and rules are extracted from his justifications of those conclusions.

For simple expert systems, the knowledge can be encoded in a simple production-rule format that treats both conditions and actions logically as propositions. More complex systems have multiple object occurrences and complex relationships. Here, standard methods of conceptual data modelling should be used as a preliminary to knowledge-base design.

As the process of knowledge engineering is becoming better understood, expert system techniques are themselves being used to automate the process. One approach, exemplified by TEIRESIAS, is based on automating the process of debugging an existing knowledge base and guiding the expert in either specifying modifications to existing rules or in adding new rules to cater for new test data. Another approach, exemplified by ROGET and XPLAIN, is to help formulate the initial development of a new knowledge base.

Software to implement an expert system must meet several criteria. It should support the knowledge representation formalism selected. It should support the chosen reasoning strategy with its own control mechanism. It should have a good user interface, and be able to integrate with other sources of data or other software.

Two basic alternatives are available. Expert system shells from commercial sources enable rapid prototyping and provide good tracing, justification and other run-time support, but also need to be matched to the representational needs. Artificial Intelligence programming languages are the next most flexible tool if a shell does not match the requirements.

EXERCISES AND PROJECTS
Chapter 4

E4.1 Prepare a feasibility report for the proposal to develop an expert system to debug computer programs in a language of your choice.

E4.2 Assuming that the above application has been assessed as feasible, collect case material of bad programs. Working in pairs, alternatively playing the roles of expert and knowledge engineer, develop an initial set of rules.

E4.3 Determine the essential objects of interest in the program debugging application and produce a conceptual analysis and proposed knowledge representation.

E4.4 Assess the software requirements for the project outlined above and establish if a suitable product is available to you. If it is, develop a prototype and assess it critically.

E4.5 Using a published expert system such as Cendrowska and Bramer's RMYCIN (see Chapter 1) as a basis, develop interactive debugging facilities like those of TEIRESIAS.

5

PLANNING, LEARNING AND INTELLIGENT TUTORING

This chapter is concerned first with problem solving and then with two aspects of learning and IKBS: machine learning applied to the problem of acquiring knowledge for knowledge-based systems, and the use of knowledge-based techniques in tutoring people. We begin by reviewing work on problem solving or planning, which contrasts with expert systems. After considering how to characterize learning, and its possible relevance to expert systems, we briefly survey different styles of learning and how they have been modelled by machine-learning programs. The application of machine learning to knowledge engineering is considered next. Finally we turn the topic of machine learning on its head and consider attempts to use knowledge based systems as tutors rather than consultants.

5.1 PLANNING AND PROBLEM SOLVING

Problem-solving is a long-standing area of research in Artificial Intelligence. In contrast to expert systems, designed as aids to human problem solving in specialized domains using a knowledge-rich approach, planning systems are applied most commonly to problems having well-defined logical structures. Problem-solving methods have often been studied in relation to unreal situations such as those of classical puzzles like the missionaries and cannibals problem or the Towers of Hanoi. However, problem-solving by planning is an area of practical importance, particularly applied to robotics, where a degree of autonomous problem-solving ability makes for more powerful and adaptable machines than those that are simply pre-programmed.

Problems like these can be characterized as having a simple specification consisting of an initial state, a final state, a series of legal moves or operations, the state changes produced by each move, and constraints on the operations. The initial and final states and intermediate states can all be represented by logic clauses or equivalent graphs. For the Towers of Hanoi problem, for example, the desired final state might be represented as:

on (1, 2)	disc (1)	peg (peg 1)
on (2, 3)	disc (2)	peg (peg 2)
on (3, peg 3)	disc (3)	peg (peg 3)

The initial state can be represented by a similar series of clauses. Such a notation can also be thought of as a graph or semantic network, as illustrated in Fig. 5.1.

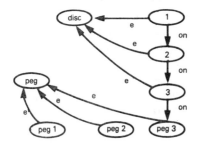

Fig. 5.1   Abstract graph for goal state in the Towers of Hanoi problem.

Two other predicates can be defined:
   The predicate 'clear', which tells if a given disc or peg has nothing on top of it, can be defined as:

clear (X) :- not (on (_, X))

The predicate 'cangoon (A, B)', which determines whether a particular disc is allowed to go above a given disc or peg (given the constraint that a disc cannot go on top of a smaller disc), can be defined as:

cangoon (A, B) :-
   disc (B),
   clear (B),
   A < B.
cangoon (A, B) :-
   peg (B),
   clear (B)

5.1.1   Operations in a problem-solving planner

In preparing a planner to solve a given problem, the possible operations must be specified. In the Towers of Hanoi problem, there is only one operation, which we could write in a unit clause as:

move (Disk, A, B)

This can be read as 'move a disk from one place to another.' However, merely stating the operation is not sufficient. What it does is specified by stating the changes it makes to the state of the problem space. 'move (Disk, A, B)' has the effect of retracting the fact 'on (Disk,)' from the current state and asserting 'on (Disk, B)'.

There are also constraints that have to be satisfied before the move can take place, in this instance on (Disc, A) and cangoon (Disc, B).

The operations are described fully to a planner if the updates made to the problem space and the constraints are specified. A planning program can use the operation descriptions and the initial and final state descriptions to discover and report a sequence of operations that will accomplish the goal. A simple planner's strategy resembles the process of searching a graph for a route from an origin to a destination. A successful plan is either a single operation that goes from an initial state to a goal state or a single step and another plan. In other words planning is a recursively defined search strategy.

Well-known planning programs in the AI literature include STRIPS and NOAH. Both are described in Daniel (1984). STRIPS was originally described in Fikes and Nilsson (1971). A Prolog planner, WARPLAN, is the basis of a case study in Klusniak and Szpakowicz (1985).

5.2 LEARNING AND KNOWLEDGE-BASED SYSTEMS

In Chapter 1, knowledge was distinguished from information as being the product of learning, and by being structured in a long-term memory. At that point, it was assumed that learning did not need to be defined. If we are to consider learning in more detail now, it is necessary to define the concept or at least to characterize it more clearly.

From a psychological point of view, learning can be said to have taken place when a permanent change in behaviour results from experience. The permanent change in behaviour is an important characteristic of learning, and contrasts with the simple problem – solving ability just described. Each time our Prolog problem solver attempts the Towers of Hanoi problem, it approaches it in the same way that it did the first time. It is not capable of benefiting from experience and making the necessary moves in the correct order straight away.

Much has been discovered about learning in animals purely by observing their behaviour in experimental tasks like finding routes in mazes or learning complex sequences of actions for rewards. However, if we are to understand learning sufficiently to build computer programs that learn, it is necessary to describe the way in which the **state** of the learner is changed to produce new behaviour, in particular how its **knowledge** is augmented or refined. We must therefore characterize learning from a logical as well as a psychological point of view.

5.2.1 What can be learned?

The knowledge that people acquire through learning includes both facts about individual entities or events and generalizations or rules. Individual facts are learned by simple memorization. Such 'learning' is particularly straightforward to implement on a machine, which doesn't require the same facts to be reiterated in the way that people do. The learning of rules and generalizations, however, can take place in several learning 'styles'.

5.2.2 Styles of learning

Carbonell, Michalski and Mitchell (1983) usefully distinguish several different styles of learning.

- Simple memorization of facts or rote learning is grouped with direct implantation of new knowledge or being programmed. This learning strategy or style is not of any real interest because it places all the responsibility and effort on the teacher instead of the learner. Applied to learning by machines, it means nothing other than programming.
- Learning from instruction. The contrast with the previous learning style is that the knowledge is provided by a source such as a book or a teacher and is expressed in some form or language which is not the same as the learner's internal representation language. As with simple memorization, a machine does not have the problem of forgetfulness that people do.
- Learning by analogy. A form of learning that requires the learner to draw more inferences on the incoming information. It involves recognition of similarity with some knowledge structure in memory and operations of abstraction and specialization.
- Learning from examples, or inductive learning. The learner has to generalize from examples, usually preselected by a teacher. This is the most extensively studied form of learning by machine.
- Learning by discovery. A more open-ended form of learning from examples, where the observations or examples are not preselected by a teacher but selected autonomously by the learner.

There are other styles of learning that do not appear in the above list, for example learning through visual imagery or through tactile or other sensorimotor experience. To date, machine-learning research has been concerned only with symbolic forms of learning.

5.2.3 The logic of learning

The different styles or strategies of learning each have their own logic. Memorization and learning from instruction amount logically to assertion of propositions. However, learning from examples is a form of inference that is not a valid logical deduction. For example, by the rules of universal specialization and *modus ponens*, we can validly infer:

$\forall$X [elephant (X) → colour (X, grey)]
elephant (clyde)

---

colour (clyde, grey)

However, the rules of deductive inference cannot account for the way we learn such generalizations as 'elephant (X) → colour (X, grey)' in the first place. We learn most such facts by being told, but somebody must have first learned them from experience. The learning of this rule follows the pattern:

elephant (clyde),	colour (clyde, grey).
elephant (dumbo),	colour (dumbo, grey).
elephant (fanta),	colour (fanta, grey).
elephant (nellie),	colour (nellie, grey).

---

elephant (X)] →   colour (X, grey).

which is not a valid deductive inference. However, it is an instance of **induction**. What distinguishes induction from deduction is that the former is not reliable. If we find an elephant whose colour is not grey, then we are no longer entitled to infer that all elephants are grey, otherwise some valid deductive inferences will lead to false conclusions.

However, most useful knowledge is corrigible in this way, and in the context of IKBS, we have already discussed methods of dealing with it by either uncertainty calculi or reasoning with defaults.

5.3 MECHANICAL INDUCTION

Several inductive reasoning programs exist, tackling different inductive learning tasks. A simple inductive learning task is to induce a generalized description of a single concept or class of objects. A **training set** of individual instances of the concept is provided, each with a description. The description is a conjunction of propositions in a predicate and argument notation that are all true of the individual object. The goal of the learner is to establish a maximally specific generalization of the concept.

Other related learning tasks are the inductive learning of **discriminant** descriptions that distinguish between concepts, and the induction of **taxonomic** descriptions relating subset and superset concepts in a hierarchy.

5.3.1 Mechanical induction strategies

A 'bottom up' strategy for inductive learning of a concept description is to start with an individual instance and hypothesize that its description is the target class description. Other instances are considered in turn, and if they do not match the current class description, the latter is modified in an attempt to obtain a description that is true for the new instance as well as those previously considered. In seeking to revise the description, various rules or operators can be applied, of which the following are examples:

1 Dropping conditions. This rule allows a class description to be generalized by dropping one of its conjuncts. It would be applied when the new instance lacks one of the properties in the current class description.

2 Disjunction introduction. Rather than drop the condition altogether, a simple term in a description may be replaced by a disjunctive term. For example, in learning the concept 'London Bus' from examples, it might be necessary to generalize the description of the colour attribute from 'colour (red)' to 'colour (red) V colour (green)' to take account of Green Line buses. A related rule is one where a conjunction of conditions is replaced by a disjunction.

3 Universal generalization. (turning constants to variables). This rule's logical schema is the opposite of the deductive rule of universal generalization:

$$F(a), F(b), F(g), F(k), \ldots \models \forall X [F(X)]$$

which is the rule we used above in generalizing that all elephants are grey.

4 Exception Introduction. This is a rule that specializes the description instead of generalizing it. It can be used if the learner is presented with negative instances of the concept as well as positive ones. For example, in learning the concept 'bird', the ability to fly is part of the description, but examples of other flying animals such as bats are cited in the training set. It is possible to add a condition (such as 'not furry') to the description to eliminate such exceptions.

One problem with these rules of generalization and specialization is that they either weaken the characteristic description or overspecialize it, and so we should prefer to use such powerful operators sparingly. Another problem is that of choosing between the rules, since different rules can be applied in similar circumstances. The order of application of different rules will also affect the result. For example, in learning of the concept 'bird', the introduction of the exception condition would not have been needed if 'lays eggs' were in the current concept description, since that is not true of bats. Finally, success in inducing a particular concept depends on the inclusion in the descriptions of individual objects in the training set all the attributes that are needed to characterize or discriminate the concept.

Learning algorithms differ in their use of particular generalizing and specializing rules, rule selection criteria, whether a bottom-up or top-down learning strategy is used, and whether negative instances are included in the training set. Several representative inductive learning programs are reviewed comparatively in Michalski (1983).

5.3.2 Learning from instruction

Much of the interest in mechanical induction must result from its tractability as a laboratory problem. It is not, however, the way that people acquire most of their knowledge. It is just too inefficient. To make all the observations that would be needed would leave too little time for the practical application of the acquired knowledge. Humans avoid 're-inventing the wheel' by passing on the knowledge they have acquired by whatever means to others through language and other forms of communication.

Recently, researchers in machine learning have been considering whether this more direct way of adding to knowledge can be applied to machines. This style of learning is related to another area of IKBS (to which we turn in the next two chapters) – natural language understanding. As in expert systems, much of the work in knowledge-based natural language understanding has assumed the prior existence of the requisite knowledge and has not considered how it is acquired. Haas and Hendrix (1983) have constructed a program that can build up a complex semantic network database from a conversation with a user who volunteers information. It is not just a matter of analysing the incoming sentences and storing away a separate representation for each. The program actively seeks to integrate the new knowledge with what it already knows, in the same way that effective human learners do.

Haas and Hendrix' program, NANOKLAUS, is armed with some preliminary knowledge ('seed concepts') and some general information about how concepts can be related. With this knowledge, it is able to accept new generalizations and where appropriate, to ask for the user to supply additional discriminating information. For example, if NANOKLAUS had already been told that a STUDENT is a PERSON, the subsequent dialogue could run:

A tutor is a person.

You're saying that anything that is a TUTOR is also a PERSON.
Is TUTOR a proper subclass of STUDENT?
no
Is TUTOR necessarily composed of entirely different members from
STUDENT?
yes
Do TUTOR and STUDENT span the set of all PERSONS?
no
Ok. Now I understand TUTOR.

5.4 KNOWLEDGE ACQUISITION FOR EXPERT SYSTEMS

The question arises: How much can state-of-the-art-machine-learning techniques contribute to the problem of knowledge acquisition for expert
systems? To date, the best example of the application of inductive learning is
the work of Michalski and Chilauski (1980), who carried out a performance
comparison of a machine-induced expert system for soya bean plant disease
diagnosis with a program whose knowledge base was expert supplied.

The problem space comprised 15 diseases of the soya bean plant and 35
plant and environmental descriptors. The expert-derived rules were captured
in dialogue with domain experts in 45 hours. To obtain the inductively
derived rules, 630 learning events were partitioned into a training set and a
testing set. An existing induction program was used to induce the rules and
took 4.5 minutes on an IBM 360. (The authors do not say how long it took to
prepare and code the test cases.)

Both the expert-supplied and inductively derived rules were used in trials
with the testing set of cases, and the inductive rules performed better: 96.7%
of diagnoses were correct first time, and the correct diagnosis was always
present in a list of likely diagnoses. The comparative figures for the expert-
derived rules were 71.8% and 96.9%. The experts' own evaluation of the
machine-induced rules was favourable, and the authors propose a knowledge-
engineering method whereby an initial rule-set is obtained inductively and
domain experts post-edit the rules obtained.

Some of the commercial expert system shell products are tools for rule
induction. An example is the 'Expert Ease' package, which uses a learning
algorithm, known as 'ID3', developed by Quinlan.

Systems for machine induction seem to work well for developing small
knowledge bases, where the cases are described by simple attribute
descriptions covering only global properties of an object and its environment.
Bundy's (1985) assessment is that such methods have limited application at
present to complex knowledge bases, and in any case, the time taken to
develop many systems by conventional human knowledge engineering is not
extravagant.

5.5 INTELLIGENT COMPUTER-AIDED INSTRUCTION AND TUTORING

Up to now, we have considered learning as a technique within IKBS. It can also be considered as an application. In Chapter 1, we noted a similarity between expert systems and systems for computer-aided instruction. The use of interactive computers in teaching is well established, but is usually provided without recourse to IKBS techniques. The standard benefits from a 'programmed learning' approach are that the student's work through a programme can be individually paced and immediate feedback can be given on the correctness of the student's responses to questions assessing comprehension of the presented material.

Several criticisms can be made of this approach, of which two are:

- Although designed for individual student use, the approach is not *student-centred*. That is, the initiative always rests with the program, and the student's role is essentially passive. In terms of our earlier list of styles of learning, it is learning from instruction, and is not genuinely interactive since the student may only attempt to answer questions posed by the system and may ask none himself.
- The ability to give genuine tutorial support to a student who makes mistakes is limited. The course writer may explicitly program the 'tutor' to recognize certain erroneous answers and present appropriate remedial text, but such a system can do no more with unanticipated errors than mark them wrong.

Interactive instructional and tutoring systems developed using IKBS techniques attempt to improve on the programmed learning approach in one or both of these respects. We consider two representative early systems: one an intelligent **instructional** system, SCHOLAR, the other an intelligent **tutoring** system, BUGGY. Both are described in Barr and Feigenbaum (1982), section C.

5.5.1 Scholar

SCHOLAR was developed by Carbonell and Collins and first reported in 1970. It was an intelligent computer-aided instruction (ICAI) system whose expertise was in South American Geography. Like programmed learning systems it could present new information and then test the student's knowledge. However, it would also allow the student to take the initiative and decline to answer the question it had set. For example, after asking the student

Approximately what is the area of Argentina?

if the student replied:

Tell me something about Peru

SCHOLAR was able not only to recognize that this was not an answer to the question, but to analyse the new request and respond appropriately. In generating its reply, it would select the most significant facts about Peru: that it is a country, its location and its capital. It could also make inferences in answering student questions. For example, if asked: 'Is Asunción hot?', it would conclude that it is, since it is part of Paraguay.

The style of dialogue supported by SCHOLAR has been described as **mixed initiative** since the student using the program can ask questions as well as submit to instruction and testing. To allow this, SCHOLAR uses two main IKBS techniques: a declarative knowledge representation – a frame system with superclass links – and a natural language 'front end' to analyse the student's input and generate responses.

The explicit knowledge representation sets the approach apart from textually oriented instructional systems; without a structured knowledge representation it would not be possible to answer questions at all. It also makes sense to use the same knowledge representation when the system is instructing or testing. A novel feature of the knowledge base was that each fact stored in it was tagged with an importance value. It was on that basis that it could select an appropriate amount of information to supply in answer to a general request like 'Tell me something about Peru' or a question like 'What is the most important difference between Peru and Paraguay'.

If the knowledge is expressed in a neutral way to support both system-initiated and student-initiated exchanges, a more sophisticated input/output subsystem is needed. For the program to recognize when a response is not an erroneous answer to a set question but a new question in its own right, it is also necessary to be able to analyse the structure and content of free-form English phrases and sentences. For these reasons, SCHOLAR incorporated a natural language interface. We take up the principles involved in such interfaces in the next three chapters, so we will not describe the approach used in SCHOLAR here.

A later ICAI system in the domain of geography, WHY (also described in Barr and Feigenbaum 1982), uses a causal model of climatology to ask the student to explain phenomena such as the heavy rainfall of the Amazon jungle. If the student does not know the answer, WHY can provide a detailed explanation in terms of a chain of intermediate causes.

5.5.2 BUGGY

Instead of providing instruction in a factual domain, BUGGY attempts to provide tutorial support for the pupil who has difficulty in primary school arithmetic. It is thus an **Intelligent Tutoring System** rather than an ICAI system. The premise behind the BUGGY approach to intelligent tutoring is that children who find arithmetic difficult are not simply unreliable in their application of the rules but are consistent in applying erroneous rules. In other words, their arithmetic procedures have bugs. The task of a good tutor is not simply to mark the pupil's work, but to find out why the pupil is going wrong and then to explain how to avoid similar errors in the future.

The sort of error BUGGY is able to correct is exemplified by a pupil giving the answer *1053* to the sum *66 + 887*. The pupil's error is to continue carrying 1 to all columns whether or not the sum of the digits in the previous column exceeds 10. The digits in the units column sum to 13, so it is correct to carry 1 to the tens column. Here the sum is fifteen, so again, there is a carry of 1 to the hundreds column. However, the sum in the hundreds column is only 9, but the pupil still carries 1 to the next column. The authors of BUGGY explain the plausibility of this answer by pointing out that many children will set a physical 'carry flag' by raising a finger, and in this case, the error is to fail to 'reset' the flag after use. BUGGY verifies that this is the child's procedure by examining several examples of both right and wrong answers. The error does not show up, for example, when no carry is required at all, as in *216 + 13 = 229*.

The strategy used by the program is to establish the student's rule from examples in the manner of a standard inductive learning program, and then when it thinks it has got the bug, to generate a new test set of examples. In looking at a single example, BUGGY accesses a knowledge base of rules of arithmetic that shows how each rule is broken down into a sequence of primitive operations. It synthesizes new rules from these primitives until it creates a rule that can generate the pupil's error. It eliminates alternative candidate rules by testing against additional examples.

When BUGGY was tested, it was found that over 40% of errors were of this consistent nature. The program was also used to help trainee teachers diagnose pupil errors by generating examples for the trainees to solve.

An important theme in Intelligent Tutoring Systems since BUGGY, has been the maintenance of a **student model**. If the program is to be able to correct errors in the student's understanding of a technique, the program must be able to represent that understanding. Thus an Intelligent Tutoring System has at least two knowledge bases, one representing the rules of the problem domain and the other representing the student. More recent research on ITS is reported in Sleeman and Brown (1984).

SUMMARY
Chapter 5

Planning is an IKBS technique that contrasts with expert systems. A planner has an axiomatic specification of the operations available in a problem domain and uses theorem proving to determine a solution to a given problem using these operations.

A planning program does not learn from experience. Each time it tackles the same problem, it rediscovers the solution. By contrast, learning involves permanent changes in the memory or ability of the learner.

Learning can take place in a number of ways: rote learning, learning from instruction, learning by analogy, inductive learning and discovery learning.

Programs have been developed that learn using each of these approaches, but the most common is inductive learning, or learning from examples.

It is often asserted that machine learning is a potential solution to the problem of knowledge acquisition for expert systems. However, inductive learning is most applicable in problem areas where the quantity and structure of knowledge is small and simple enough for knowledge acquisition not to be a bottleneck.

Learning from instruction is more characteristic of human learning, since people do not have the time to learn all they know from direct experience. Some experimental systems have been constructed which show that it may be a feasible approach to knowledge acquisition.

IKBS techniques are also associated with instruction and tutoring. Conventional approaches to programmed learning provide some benefits of feedback and individually paced learning, but are inflexible.

Intelligent Computer-Aided Instruction (ICAI) systems are usually mixed-initiative, and use a declarative knowledge base both to generate instruction and test questions and to respond to student enquiries.

Intelligent Tutoring Systems (ITS) have an explicit model of the student's understanding of the rules of some discipline which they use in order to provide genuine diagnostic feedback on the sources of student errors.

EXERCISES AND PROJECTS Chapter 5

E5.1 State the initial and final conditions, permissible moves and constraints for the missionaries and cannibals problem in Prolog clauses. (The task is for three missionaries to transport three cannibals across a river in a two-seat canoe without allowing any of themselves to be outnumbered by cannibals. It is permissible to leave a number of cannibals unsupervised on one side of the river.)

E5.2   Use the WARPLAN program (Klusniak and Szpakowicz, 1984 or Coelho, Cotta and Pereira, 1982) to implement and test your solution to the missionaries and cannibals problem and the Towers of Hanoi. (Note that in WARPLAN, constraints are represented explicitly, and not simply built into the definition of allowable operations).

6

NATURAL LANGUAGE UNDERSTANDING

The present chapter reviews the fundamentals of natural language processing by computer. We start by examining the motivations for computer understanding of natural language, then the basic principles, before looking at the problem of syntactic analysis of English. One approach to syntactic parsing, the Definite Clause Grammar (DCG), is examined in detail.

We shall use the term 'natural language understanding' and its abbreviation, NLU, to refer to any effort to analyse the meaning of utterances or texts in natural languages. The creation of new utterances or texts is referred to as 'generation' or 'production' (although as we shall see below, 'generation' has a specialized and slightly different meaning in linguistics). We will have less to say about production than about understanding, reflecting the relative effort devoted to the two problems in the past.

6.1 MOTIVATION

There are two kinds of reason for wanting to build computer programs that appear to 'understand' or 'generate' natural language.

One is practical: where the NLU capability is either an essential or desirable feature of a computer system that performs a useful function. It is this practical purpose for natural language understanding that belongs to the field we have called IKBS.

The range of applications for computer understanding of natural language (NLU) is increasing all the time. Earliest and perhaps most obvious is machine translation. Obtaining information from computer databases in one's native language has also been a long-standing application. Programming in natural language has been proposed, but there is little to show for such efforts. More recently, applications in office automation, such as advanced word-processing aids – grammar and style correctors, for example – have been proposed and are currently under development.

The second reason is theoretical: having a computer process language is a way of testing theories developed within the various human sciences whose object of study is language. This research is not so much IKBS as computational linguistics or psycholinguistics or more generally 'cognitive science'. Nevertheless, techniques developed from such motives may be put to practical use. In this chapter, we will consider the general problem of determining the structure of natural language texts or utterances and assigning them a representation of their meaning.

6.2 PROCESSING NATURAL LANGUAGE

When we first attempt a functional description of a computational process,

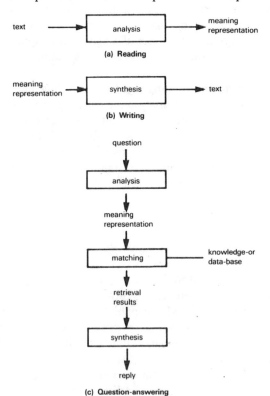

Fig. 6.1   Schematic view of some linguistic processes.

we specify the inputs and the corresponding outputs of the process. To get a clear picture of computer NLU, we shall need to do the same. Figure 6.1 shows in schematic form a number of linguistic processes.

In the case of question answering, the input and the output are clear enough – we would expect both a question and a reply to take the form of a string of sounds or characters. For the time being, we will make the simplifying assumption that natural language processing applies to written or typed input and output and not speech.

In all three diagrams, however, we also have other inputs, outputs, or intermediate forms of data which we have called 'meaning representations'. One of the major problems in natural language understanding is that there is no widespread agreement on what a meaning representation is. Naturally each practical system incorporates a particular conception of what a meaning is, but often this is closely tied to a particular application task, and does not imply that there is a general theory of meaning for natural language.

There are several different aspects of meaning:

1　Representational or propositional meaning is concerned with the structure of the logical proposition underlying a sentence. This is perhaps the most fundamental aspect of meaning for most purposes. It will normally be expressed in one or other of the formalisms for knowledge representation introduced in Chapter 3.

2　Referential meaning is concerned with correctly identifying the real world entities referred to by nouns, and more problematically, by pronouns.

3　Paraphrase: An important feature of human languages is the ability to express the same propositional content in different ways. This is encouraged normally as a stylistic practice, and can involve the use of synonyms, substituting descriptions for words, or using different syntactic forms.

4　Ambiguity occurs when the same sentence or phrase has two or more distinct meanings. Most ambiguous sentences have a preferred meaning, and determining what this is is termed **resolving** the ambiguity.

5　Pragmatic meaning is concerned with identifying the effect the speaker intends to achieve by his utterance. In speech, for example, it is unusual to give an instruction in the imperative mood, since that might be taken as seeming too aggressive. A question, such as 'Would you mind putting your cigarette out?' is more appropriate in most circumstances.

The list is not exhaustive, but any NLU system must attend at least to aspects **1** to **4**, and systems that conduct a dialogue with a user need to deal with **5**.

6.3 ANALYSIS AND PARSING

The content of the boxes labelled 'analysis' in the processes of reading and question-answering in Fig. 6.1 is the topic of the rest of this chapter. The ultimate goal is to produce a meaning representation from an input text.

As we saw in the discussion of 'frames' in Chapter 3, one purpose of a meaning representation is to identify correctly the respective roles of the various participants in an action or event. We can clearly see the need for this if we consider the active and passive sentence forms for representing the same proposition. The sentences

John kicked the computer

and

The computer was kicked by John

can both be represented by

```
(ACTION : STRIKE 1
  (ACTOR : JOHN 1)
  (PATIENT : COMPUTER 1)
  (INSTRUMENT : FOOT 1))
(STATE : OWN 1
  (OWNER : JOHN 1)
  (OWNEE : FOOT 1))
```

or by equivalent logic clauses or perhaps a semantic network.

While the propositional meaning is identical, the grammatical structure is different in both cases. In addition, a traditional grammatical analysis would identify 'John' as the subject of the first sentence, but 'the computer' as the subject of the second. We thus have to make a distinction between the grammatical subject of a sentence and its logical subject.

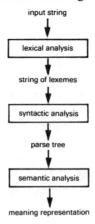

Fig. 6.2 Levels of linguistic analysis.

6.4 LEVELS OF LINGUISTIC ANALYSIS

As is conventional in linguistics, Fig. 6.2 shows the processing taking place on a number of levels.

Lexical analysis is concerned with identifying from the input stream of characters the basic units which will be further analysed in the next level. We can think of these as words, but lexical analysis goes beyond merely identifying word boundaries to further analysing words into roots and affixes (affix is a generic term for both prefixes and suffixes), where appropriate. The higher levels of analysis will use both the roots and affixes (which convey such information as tense and number) as basic units. We can use the term 'lexeme' to cover both roots and affixes, hence lexical analysis.

This stage of processing is clearly simplified when we consider only written text. In processing speech, what we have called lexical analysis is in fact two distinct levels of analysis: phonetic analysis, concerned with identifying the basic units of sound, called 'phonemes' (which are roughly the equivalent of written letters), and morphological analysis, concerned with roots and affixes.

Syntax is the next level of analysis. Here we are concerned with the grouping of lexical units into phrases and thence into higher-level units such as clauses or sentences. The analysis we do at this stage may be exemplified by the tree diagram and corresponding labelled bracketing in Fig. 6.3.

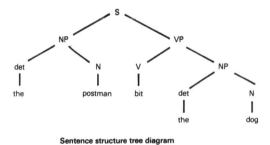

Sentence structure tree diagram

s(np (det (the), n(postman)), vp (v (bit), np (det (the), n (dog))))

Labelled bracketing for the same sentence

Fig. 6.3   Constituent structure analysis.

Such analysis has long been part of the stock-in-trade of linguists and language teachers.

What is more recent is the idea that rules for deriving such an analysis can be specified explicitly yet economically. This was first done in the 1950's by the linguists Harris and Chomsky (and was immediately adopted for the description of computer languages). Figure 6.4 shows a set of grammar rules which can be applied to give the structures shown in Fig. 6.3 for the sentence 'The postman bit the dog'.

Identifying the correct syntactic structure for a sentence is known as parsing and the output of this process is normally a parse tree. The parse tree is the input to the stage of semantic interpretation. As we are not committed to a particular form of meaning representation, we will ignore details of this last processing stage for the time being. We note, however, that our main reason for doing the syntax analysis is that the structure modelled in the parse tree is relevant to the meaning structure. We explore some aspects of semantics in Chapter 7.

6.4.1 Syntactic rules

We have introduced some example rules of syntax and placed syntax and parsing in context. Before we can turn to the examination of a method of parsing, we need to explore the nature of these rules and of grammars.

The first three rules in Fig. 6.4 are syntactic rules, and the last four are lexical rules.

```
S     →   NP, VP
NP    →   det, N
VP    →   V, NP

V     →   bit
det   →   the
N     →   postman
N     →   dog
```

Fig. 6.4 Sample grammar rules.

The rules in Fig. 6.4 will in fact permit us to generate only two sentences:

The postman bit the dog.

and

The dog bit the postman.

However, the symbols for the lexical units, 'V', 'det' and 'N' in fact represent whole classes of words. For 'bit', we could substitute 'ate', 'kicked', 'nipped', 'saw', 'liked', 'bought' and many others and get sentences of identical structure (although different meanings). We can apply the same principle to the N class, substituting any of literally thousands of nouns where we had 'dog' and 'postman', and to a lesser extent with 'the'. Here there are fewer alternatives: 'a', 'any', 'some', 'that', 'this' and perhaps a few others. By thus expanding our lexical rules to permit the selection of all of the transitive verbs, nouns and determiners (articles) in a typical English dictionary, we would be able to account for the structure of a prodigious (but still finite) number of rather boring sentences.

In addition to allowing alternative lexical rules, we can do the same with the syntactic rules. An alternative VP (verb phrase) rule might be:

```
VP      →      copula Adj
```

with corresponding lexical rules including

```
copula  →      is
Adj     →      fat
Adj     →      lazy
```

An alternative NP (noun phrase) rule might be:

```
NP      →      npr
```

where

```
npr     →      John
npr     →      Mary
```

These alternative rules, like the lexical rules, multiply the number of possible sentences in the language to a large, but still finite number. An important feature of most interesting languages (natural and artificial) is that their sentences may contain **recursive** structures. Three such structures in English are:

1 *Co-ordination*

```
NP           →      NP, conj, NP
```

e.g. John and James and Joe and the dog. . . .

2 *Adjectival modification*

```
Nominal    →      Adj, Nominal
Nominal    →      N
```

e.g. dirty great big fat greasy blob.

3 *Relative clauses*

```
NP      →      det, Nominal, Rel
Rel     →      'that', VP
VP      →      verb, NP
```

e.g. The dog that chased the cat that killed the rat that ate the poison

In practice, of course, people do not use the full formal capability of language for infinite recursion, but taken together, alternative lexical rules, alternative syntactic rules and recursive rules allow an enormous number of sentences to be described by a very simple rule formalism.

6.4.2 Generative grammar

The rules above are said to **generate** the sentences of a language, and a grammar which is written using such rules is called a **generative grammar**. The term 'generative' sometimes causes confusion, seeming to imply that in some way the grammar shows how the utterances or sentences of the language are created in a dynamic sense. What we termed 'synthesis' in Fig. 6.1 is not the same as 'generation' in the technical sense in which it is used in linguistics. In the processes modelled by those schematic diagrams, we used 'synthesis' to denote the process of **translating** from a meaning representation into a text or utterance. This implies that what we want to say in the language is available already in some other form. By contrast, the rules in a generative grammar do not show how the sentences of a language are related to anything else, merely how the elements of which they are built are grouped. In order to synthesize any real sentences, we have to add some procedure for selecting which lexical and syntactic rules to employ from the alternatives available. This might of course take the form of a procedure to select words and structures at random, a procedure whose sole usefulness would be as a check on the correctness of the set of rules.

Chomsky made a clear distinction between the point of view of linguistics on the one hand and that of the information processing view of language on the other: He said that the former was interested in a theory of **competence** in the use of language, whereas the latter was interested in a theory of **performance**.

Here, we are interested in performance, but in a way which incorporates a theory of competence. A computer program which analyses or synthesizes natural language text will employ as an essential component a database of linguistic knowledge which will include the rules of grammar of the language being processed.

Confusingly, there are those in the various fields of language study who either reject the need for a distinction between competence and performance or are not interested in the former, and who use the term 'generation' where we have used 'synthesis'. One way out of the confusion is to remember that if it is said that a *grammar* generates something, the specialized linguistic sense of the word is being used, whereas if *system* or *speaker* is the subject, then the looser sense is intended.

6.4.3 Types of generative grammar

The grammar rules we have employed up to now in examples have always been of the same type. All rules in a generative grammar have as their essential form a left-hand side and a right-hand side, separated by an arrow whose meaning can be read as 'can be re-written as'. In our examples, we have also observed a restriction that the left-hand side of the rules is, in every case, a single symbol, and the right-hand side always consists of one or more symbols.

This type of grammar is known as a **Type 2** grammar, or a **context-free** grammar. It is one of four types of grammar identified by Chomsky on the basis of the formal properties of its rules and of the corresponding languages that can be generated. Context-free grammars are of particular interest for two reasons:

1   The analysis that they give of sentences is the familiar tree structure which shows the hierarchical grouping of phrases.
2   There are well-known parsing strategies available for them.

It has, however, been argued by Chomsky that context-free grammars (CFGs) are inadequate for the description of natural languages. It is possible to assign phrase structures to any sentence in a language like English, but Chomsky argues that using only context-free rules will miss out significant regularities in the language. The sort of language features concerned are agreement between nouns and verbs, co-ordination, and the relatedness of active and passive, declarative and interrogative sentences. These regularities can be described by a more simple set of rules if we make a distinction between the **surface structure** and the **deep structure** of a sentence. The latter is an analysis which is arguably closer to the meaning of the sentence. It can be argued that the passive sentence:

The tape drive was fixed by John

should have the same structural analysis as the corresponding active sentence:

John fixed the tape drive

The question:

Who fixed the tape drive?

should be related in its analysis to the statement:

Someone fixed the tape drive.

Transformational grammar

A grammar which employs a **base** set of rules for generating deep structures and a further set of **transformational** rules showing how they are related to surface structures is known as a **transformational grammar**.

6.5   PARSING WITH GENERATIVE GRAMMAR

For languages described by context-free grammars, there are a number of standard approaches to parsing, described extensively in the literature on computer languages and compilers. A 'top-down' parser starts by attempting to satisfy first the highest-level phrase structure rules (the 'sentence' or 'program' rule according to the language). Where in the right-hand side of a rule there is a symbol (called a **non-terminal**) which occurs on the left-hand side of other rules, the latter rules become sub-goals. Whenever a symbol occurs which is a **terminal**, the parser attempts to match with the next symbol from the input stream. If the match fails, alternative rules can be tried. This may involve **backtracking** up to alternative higher-level rules. A parser which employs backtracking is said to be **nondeterministic**, whereas one which does not may be described as deterministic.

Not all context-free grammars can be parsed deterministically, although some can be rewritten so that the right-hand side of each rule starts off with a terminal symbol. It is a fertile research area in the psychology of language whether human language processing is deterministic.

Some context-free grammars cannot even be parsed nondeterministically by the top-down approach. This occurs where there is a 'left-recursive' rule: one in which the first symbol on the right-hand side is the same as that on the left-hand side. A case in point is the rule for coordination which was given above. The problem here is that when such a rule becomes the goal, it calls itself as a subgoal recursively before the rest of the right-hand side has the opportunity to test for a particular terminal. For a top-down parser, the only solution is to rewrite the rule in such a way that it either becomes right recursive, or an iteration replaces the left recursion. Unfortunately, it is then more difficult to build a parse tree which analyses the phrase structure correctly.

Transformational–generative grammars are more difficult to parse, being more thoroughly nondeterministic. A number of such systems have been constructed, most notably by Petrick and his associates at IBM, but the NLU community has preferred alternative approaches.

6.5.1 Augmented transition networks (ATNs)

The most widely used formalism for what we could call 'computational grammars' is known as the Augmented Finite State Transition Network. In this formalism, the **description** of the language is merged to some extent with a **procedural** account of how to process it. The approach is extensively described in Chapters 5 and 7 and in Appendix D of Winograd (1983). The reader who proposes to specialize in the Natural Language area within IKBS should make a study of the ATN, but we shall not examine it here.

The approach we are following below (the DCG) is compared with the ATN in Pereira and Warren (1980). As they point out, the DCG is more descriptive, while treating 'transformational' features of syntax in a similar way.

6.6 DEFINITE CLAUSE GRAMMAR

The Definite Clause Grammar (DCG) is the name given to a formalism for representing grammars in a rule format that is an extension of the context-free notation, but has the power of a transformational grammar. A DCG is an analyser as well as being a grammar, since it constitutes a Prolog program.

The DCG can be written directly in standard Prolog, but for efficiency, it is necessary to include working variables as additional parameters in the clauses. To overcome this problem, a special **grammar rule notation** has been devised which hides this from the writer. Rules in the grammar rule notation are **preprocessed** when the file is consulted, into the standard Prolog form. The latter is discussed fully in Pereira and Warren (1980), and so we shall base our discussion of DCG's entirely on the grammar rule notation.

A number of example DCG grammars are discussed below. For reference, Fig. 6.10 shows a sample of input and output for four of them. The five grammars have been 'consulted' from the files DCG1 to DCG5 and correspond to the grammars listed in Fig. 6.5 to 6.9 respectively.

Figure 6.5 shows a very simple grammar in DCG notation. You will notice that the syntax rules are exactly as their CFG equivalent. The grammar rule preprocessor translates the set of rules in such a way that the top-level sentence goal has two parameters, the input list of words, and a working variable. If this goal is called with the following actual parameters, Prolog will report success:

sentence ([john, kicked, the, cat], _).

Failure will be reported if the first parameter is any list which cannot be recognized by the grammar.

```
/* _____ */
/* DCG1 recognizer for simple active sentences.    */
/* _____ */
sentence → noun_phrase, verb_phrase.
noun_phrase → det, common_noun.
noun_phrase → proper_noun.
verb_phrase → verb, noun_phrase.
/* lexical rules _____ */
det → [the].
det → [a].
common_noun → [dog].
common_noun → [cat].
common_noun → [girl].
common_noun → [boy].
proper_noun → [jane].
proper_noun → [john].
proper_noun → [rover].

verb → [kicked].
verb → [kissed].
verb → [killed].
```

Fig. 6.5 Definite clause grammar recognizer.

The DCG shown in Fig. 6.5 is a **recognizer** of sentences of the language defined rather than a parser. It simply reports whether a string of words is or is not a valid sentence, but it does not give an analysis of the sentence.

Lexical rules

Square brackets within the right-hand side of a rule mean that the goal on the left-hand side is satisfied if the next item from the input stream is identical with the atom inside the brackets. If the goal is satisfied in this way, the hidden scanner will advance past the matched word. A rule which specifies only an exact match with a word is known as a lexical rule.

6.6.1   The DCG as a parser

It is a simple matter to turn the recognizer into a parser. The parse tree, represented as a structure like the labelled bracketing shown in Fig. 6.3, can be made an argument of the sentence goal. The DCG shown in Fig. 6.6 shows how this is done. After preprocesing, the sentence goal has an additional parameter to the two of the recognizer. The *first* argument is for the output structural analysis. To test the parser given in Fig. 6.6, we could supply a top-level goal:

sentence (T, [rover, kissed, the, cat], _).

and Prolog would respond:

T = s(np(npr(rover)), vp(v(kissed), np(det(the), cn(cat)))).

```
/* _____ */
/* DCG2 parser for simple active sentences.              */
/* Parses the sentences recognized by DCG1.              */
/* _____ */

sentence (s (NP, VP)) → noun_phrase (NP), verb_phrase (VP).
noun_phrase (np(DET, N)) → det (DET), common_noun (N).
noun_phrase (np (N)) → proper_noun (N).
verb_phrase (vp (V, NP)) → verb (V), noun_phrase (NP).

/* lexical rules (sample)_____ */

det (det (the)) → [the].
common_noun (cn (dog)) → [dog].
proper_noun (npr (jane)) → [jane].
verb (v (kicked)) → [kicked].
```

Fig. 6.6   Definite clause grammar as a parser.

When the sentence goal is called, the outermost pair of brackets in the structure will be labelled 's'. At this time, the detailed contents of the constituent parts will not be known. These are left as the variables NP and VP. The variable NP will be instantiated with a structure when one of the alternative *noun phrase* goals is proved.

As the Prolog proof procedure proceeds from top down, left to right through the rules, the parse structure will be built from the outside in. At each stage in the parse, structures will be passed between procedures with some parts instantiated and others left as variables. The general guideline is that the structure argument in each rule bears the label for the constituent on the left-hand side of the rule, and the right-hand components are represented as variables. The same principle is followed with the lexical rules so that each *terminal* item in the structure is also labelled.

6.6.2 Lexical rules

We can simplify the individual lexical entries by having a rule building the structure of each word class, and standard Prolog clauses listing the individual words, as shown in Fig. 6.7.

```
/* _____ */
/* Lexical rules.                                        */
/* A single rule for each lexical class enables a simpler */
/* format for the individual dictionary entries, which are */
/* encoded as standard Prolog clauses.                   */
/* _____ */

det (det (W)) →, {is_determiner (D)}.

is_determiner (the).
is_determiner (a).

common_noun (cn (W)) → [W], {is_noun (W)}.

is_noun (dog).
is_noun (girl).

proper_noun (npr (W)) → [W], {is_name (W)}.

is_name (jane).
is_name (rover).

verb (v (W)) → [W], {is_verb (W)}.

is_verb (kicked).
is_verb (kissed).
```

Fig. 6.7 Lexical rules in a DCG.

In the rules, we have employed further variants on the notation. In the square brackets, we have used Prolog variables instead of atoms to represent the lexical item consumed from the input stream, and we have enclosed additional Prolog goals in braces (curly brackets). The braces may contain any conjunction of Prolog goals and can thus impose arbitrary conditions on any variables elsewhere in the rule. In these lexical rules the condition is employed so that the individual dictionary entries can be cast as simple facts rather than as rules.

6.7 DCG TREATMENT OF CONTEXT-SENSITIVITY

The DCG notation extends the representational capabilities beyond that of the CFG by using arguments for purposes other than structure building. Figure 6.8 shows a DCG that is able to insist on the correct agreement in number between a subject noun and the main verb in a sentence. It also recognizes the present and simple past tenses and records the tense and the root form of the verb in the parse.

```
/* _____ */
/* DCG4 parser for simple active sentences.                  */
/* Requires subject nouns and verbs to agree                 */
/* in number.                                                */
/* _____ */
sentence (s (NP, VP)) → noun_phrase (Num, NP),
                        verb_phrase (Num, VP).
noun_phrase (Num, np (DET, N)) → det (DET),
                        common_noun (Num, N).
noun_phrase (sing, np (N)) → proper_noun (N).
verb_phrase (Num, vp ((V, Tns), NP)) → verb (Num, TNS, V),
                        noun_phrase (N2, NP).

/* lexical rules (examples) _____ */

det (det(W)) → [W], {is_determiner (D)}.

is_determiner (the).

common_noun (sing, cn (W)) → [W], {is_noun (W)}.
common_noun (plur, cn (W)) → [W], {pl (S, W), is_noun (S)}.

pl (dog, dogs).
is_noun (dog).

proper_noun (npr (W)) → [W], {is_name (W)}.

is_name (john).

verb (plur, pres, v(W)) → [W], {is_verb (W)}.
verb (sing, pres, v (W)) → [W], {pl (W, W1), is_verb (W1)}.
verb (Num, past, v (W)) → [W1], {past (W, W1), is_verb (W)}.

pl (kicks, kick).
is_verb (kick).
past (kick, kicked).
```

Fig. 6.8 DCG with number agreement and tense.

6.7.1 Active and passive

Another non-context-free feature of language which the DCG can handle is
the building of a standard 'deep' parse tree for different 'surface' sentence
structures. In the example which follows in Fig. 6.9, we take the deep
structure to be the same as the active surface structure, but in practice, a deep
structure would be different in form. To make it easier to see how the
substitutions of the grammatical and logical subject and object are made, we
have reverted to the sample grammar of Fig. 6.5–6.7.

```
/* _____ */
/* DCG5 – Parser for active and passives.                   */
/* For simplicity, ignores tense and number.                */
/* _____ */

sentence (S) → noun_phrase (Subj),
                verb_phrase (Subj, S).

noun_phrase (np (DET, N)) →
                det (DET),
                common_noun (N).
noun_phrase (np (N)) →
                proper_noun (N).

verb_phrase (Subj, s (Obj, vp (V, Subj))) →
                [was],
                verb (V),
                [by],
                noun_phrase (Obj).
verb_phrase (Subj, s(Subj, vp (V, Obj))) →
                verb (V),
                noun_phrase (Obj).

/* lexical rules (as for dcg3, Fig. 6.7)                    */
```

Fig. 6.9   DCG parser for actives and passives.

With the possibility of the passive construction being used, the **logical**
subject (normally the agent of the action) cannot be identified until the **grammatical** subject has been completely analysed. The first clue to the use of the
passive voice comes when we encounter, within the verb phrase, the use of the
auxiliary 'was'. By that time, if the sentence goal was

sentence (s(NP, VP)) → noun_phrase (NP), verb_phrase (VP)

as before, the NP would be instantiated to the grammatical subject. In
Prolog, of course, once a variable has been instantiated, it cannot change its
value so long as it remains in scope. Therefore, if we come across the passive
verb form and later 'by' which marks the 'agent' of an action, we cannot
change our mind and substitute a new value for the logical subject.

The solution is not to become committed to the logical subject until its
value is certain.

Accordingly, we don't build the grammatical subject identified by the initial noun_phrase goal into the structure argument of the sentence goal directly. Instead it is passed to the verb_phrase goal which now has to return not only the analysis of the VP but also that of the sentence as a whole. To see how this is done for each of the two sentence forms, we can examine the second formal parameter in the corresponding verb_phrase goals (Fig. 6.9).

```
CProlog version 1.5
| ?- [dcg1].
dcg1 consulted 1168 bytes 0.900001 sec.

yes
| ?- sentence ([the, boy, kissed, rover], _).

yes
| ?- sentence ([rover, licked, the, boy], _).

no
| ?- [-dcg2].
dcg2 reconsulted 1944 bytes 0.916667 sec.

yes
| ?- sentence ([T, [the, boy, kissed, rover], _).

T = s(np(det(the), cn(boy)), vp(v(kissed), np(npr(rover))))

yes
| ?- [-dcg4].
dcg4 reconsulted 1464 bytes 1.550001 sec.

yes
| ?- sentence (T, [the, dog, kills, the, cats], _).

T = s(np(det(the), cn(dog)), vp((v(kills), pres), np(det(the), cn

yes
| ?- sentence (T, [the, dogs, kill, the, cat], _).

T = s(np(det(the), cn(dogs)), vp((v(kill),pres), np(det(the), cn

yes
| ?- sentence (T, [the, dogs, kills, the, cats], _).

no
| ? [-dcg5].
dcg5 reconsulted 444 bytes 1.166666 sec.

yes
| ?- sentence (T, [a, dog, kissed, jane], _).

T = s(np(det(a), n(dog)), vp(v(kissed), np(npr(jane))))

yes
| ?- sentence (T,[jane, was, kissed, by, a, dog], _).

T = s(np(det(a), n(dog)), vp(v(kissed), np(npr(jane))))

yes
```

Fig. 6.10 Sample DCG input and output.

The examples presented here show the barest elements of the DCG approach to parsing natural language. Pereira and Warren (1980) give a more elaborate grammar which can cope with much of the complexity of verb phrases, including the auxiliary system, and also with relative clauses. They also show how a DCG parser can directly construct formulae of predicate logic instead of a linguistically oriented deep structure.

FURTHER READING

We have examined one approach to computer understanding of natural language in some detail. It is only one of many. The reader wishing to sample the others could begin by consulting Winograd (1983), especially Chapter 7. A good follow-up collection of chapters on individual approaches is King (1983).

SUMMARY Chapter 6

Computer understanding of natural language is studied for two reasons: to create natural interfaces to other computer systems, and to advance the study of human language use.

Linguistic processes can be viewed as translations between the external forms of spoken or written language and internal meaning representations.

More attention has been given to the analysis of language and especially **parsing**, than to the synthesis or production of new utterances.

Linguistic analysis is considered conventionally to take place on a number of different levels.

The syntax of a language can be described formally in a generative grammar.

There are a number of types of generative grammar. Of these, context-free grammars are easy to parse, but miss some significant generalizations about natural language structure.

A Definite Clause Grammar (DCG) can account for context-sensitive features by embedding subscripts and structures in context-free rules.

A DCG is at the same time a declarative representation of the syntax of a language and an executable Prolog program. It can produce either a 'deep' syntactic parse or direct translation to a semantic representation such as predicate calculus.

SUGGESTIONS FOR PRACTICAL WORK Chapter 6

E6.1   Amalgamate the DCG's listed in Fig 7.8 and 7.9 to deal with active/passive and agreement and tense simultaneously.

E6.2   Study the sample DCG listed in Pereira and Warren (1980), and implement it with an extensive dictionary.

E6.3   Develop a more extended treatment of noun phrases, accounting for nouns used as modifiers (e.g. 'boiler house', 'motor car spares shop') and for possessives such as 'The old man's father's best suit'.

7

SEMANTICS IN NATURAL
LANGUAGE UNDERSTANDING

This chapter is concerned with how the conceptual meaning of the sentences in a text can be represented, and how semantic knowledge must be used to guide or constrain other aspects of language processing. The problems of reference and sense resolution that pervade all language understanding are discussed, and approaches to their solution using semantics are outlined. We give extended consideration to a theory of human natural language understanding that is based heavily on real-world knowledge and places specifically linguistic knowledge, such as that of syntax, in the background. Finally, the integration of syntax and semantics is considered in two approaches to language understanding.

As we point out in Fig. 6.2, syntactic parsing is not the end point of linguistic analysis. There are several aspects of meaning to consider. We listed five in Chapter 6: propositional meaning, reference, paraphrase, ambiguity and pragmatics. The first two may be thought of as the 'core' of the meaning of a sentence: the structures of the underlying logical proposition, and the identities of the individual objects about which or whom the proposition is asserted or queried. The representations outlined in Chapter 3 are able to represent both of these aspects of meaning. Later in this chapter, we shall be looking at approaches that use frame-like and logic representations respectively.

7.1 AMBIGUITY AND PARAPHRASE

These two aspects of meaning are concerned with the relationships between different sentences and propositions. We need to know when two sentences are **paraphrases,** i.e. when they are equivalent in meaning, if we are to make any inferences from an assertion or in attempting to answer a question. Two sentences are paraphrases if they are given the same logical representation. The opposite of paraphrase is **polysemy** or ambiguity. A single sentence is ambiguous if it has two or more logical representations. Four classes of ambiguity can be identified:

1 **Reference** ambiguity exists where a word or phrase may refer to one of several individuals or objects that have previously been mentioned. This often occurs with pronouns, but also with descriptive noun phrases.

2 **Structural** (or syntactic) ambiguity occurs where a sentence has two or more syntactic parses, as in the well-known wartime headline:

   Allies push bottles up German rear.

   In this sentence, the alternative readings arise because both 'push' and 'bottles' can serve as either a noun or a verb (at least in the colloquial language of newspaper headlines).

3 **Quantifier scope** ambiguity occurs when there is no direct syntactic ambiguity, but there are two or more logical quantifiers which can have different scopes. The classical example is:

   Every man loves some woman.

   which can be taken to mean 'There is one single woman who is loved by every man' or 'Each man loves a (probably different) woman'.

4 **Sense** ambiguity occurs where a sentence has two or more distinct logical readings. Where this is not also accompanied by structural ambiguity, we call it 'word sense ambiguity'. There are many words that have multiple senses, for instance 'set' has over 100 distinct meanings in one dictionary. Another oft-cited example is the word 'bank' which can have either a 'river bank' sense or a 'savings bank' sense (and a sense as a verb).

The following pair of sentences shows how both reference and word-sense ambiguity can arise:

   Tom carried a bag of gold coins to the bank. He threw it in.

Based on linguistic rules alone, it is impossible to say whether 'bank' in the first sentence refers to a river bank or finance house. In the second sentence, we also have the reference ambiguity of 'it'. In this instance 'it' is serving as an **anaphoric** pronoun, that is, one that refers to an object which is the referent of a noun phrase in the preceding discourse, in either the same or a previous sentence. (Much less common are **cataphoric** pronouns, which refer to objects that are going to be mentioned later, and **exophoric** pronouns that refer to objects or individuals that exist in the extra-linguistic environment – for example 'you' is nearly always used in this way.)

7.1.1 Resolution of ambiguity

There are several humorous ambiguous sentences that are well-used in the literature. In addition to 'Allies push' another example is:

If the baby doesn't thrive on cows' milk, boil it.

These are funny because they are unusual, and because a mischievous interpretation can be derived on purely formal grounds, whereas the application of common-sense knowledge leaves only one sensible reading. Common-sense knowledge, which we apply all the time in understanding language, is being used here to **resolve** the ambiguity.

Sometimes this common-sense knowledge can easily be cast as linguistic knowledge. We can, for example, say that the object of the very 'boil' must be a noun that represents either a liquid or an item of food. 'Milk' would satisfy such a test but 'baby' would not. Linguists have long found such **lexical sub-categorization** useful even in syntax. Broader subclasses of nouns, such as *animate, mass* and *count* have a direct bearing on purely syntactic phenomena such as agreement.

The pair of sentences we used earlier to illustrate reference and word-sense ambiguity together:

Tom carried a bag of gold coins to the bank. He threw it in.

illustrates several aspects of common-sense inference in language understanding.

- Normally we do resolve ambiguity. After reading or hearing the first of these sentences, most people would agree that the bank referred to is the financial kind of bank, probably because of the reference to gold coins. Also, on purely syntactic grounds, 'it' could refer to either the bag or the bank that have both been mentioned in the previous sentence. The correct resolution here is quite clear, since a bank (of either kind) cannot be thrown.
- Usually we are not aware of even having to decide which is the intended meaning. This would certainly be the case in the resolution of the reference of 'it'.
- The resolution of ambiguity can be wrong, and we often find that we have to change it in the light of later information. Once the second example sentence has been read, it is much more likely that the bank referred to in the first was a river bank, since throwing something in is more likely to be done to a river than to a bank.
- Common-sense reasoning can be applied also to fill in part of the sense of a sentence that has been omitted by the speaker (or writer). The logical predicate that constitutes the sense of 'threw' takes three arguments, which we can call the actor (or subject), i.e. Tom, the object, i.e. the bag, and the destination. The destination was specified

only partially using the preposition 'in' as the complement of the verb. However, our common-sense reasoning and the resolutions made of other potential ambiguities can identify the value for this argument as the river. In some linguistic theories, the logical arguments of a verb are described as its **conceptual cases**. ('Conceptual' to distinguish their semantic nature from the syntactic cases used in languages such as Latin). Such theories view the meaning representation of a verb as a frame (cf. Chapter 3).

7.2   A THEORY AND MODEL OF CONCEPTUAL UNDERSTANDING

The research goal of some workers in natural language understanding is to establish a comprehensive model of what it means to understand language. Such research extends its concerns beyond the basic syntactic unit of the sentence to texts of any length, and to the way in which the reading of a text involves accessing and changing structures in memory. Thus the inspiration for this work comes more from psychology than from linguistics.

The best-known work in this field is that of the Yale Artificial Intelligence Project under the direction of Roger Schank. Schank's work first came to prominence in 1972 with the publication of his theory of **Conceptual Dependency**.

Conceptual dependency is essentially a meaning-representation formalism. As such it is one candidate for the outcome of the multi-level linguistic analysis shown in Fig. 6.2. Its strong point is that it gives a standard representation to the conceptual content of an utterance no matter what lexical choices have been made. In other words, it provides a solution to the paraphrase problem mentioned at the beginning of this chapter.

The Conceptual Dependency (henceforward 'CD') structures have been employed in representing the meaning of stories and questions about them. The practical demonstrations of understanding implemented by Schank's students have included question-answering, summarizing and translating stories. In the course of the work on question-answering particularly, it has been clear that in addition to representing the propositional content of the story, an understander brings to bear much real-world knowledge to the task. The Yale school's work has been concerned largely with the organization of this knowledge and of the inferences that are drawn in processing.

7.3   CONCEPTUAL DEPENDENCY

A CD representation is a *graph* whose nodes are entities drawn from four basic conceptual categories:

1 **Picture producers** (PPs) correspond roughly to nouns, but the name is intended to evoke their psychological function rather than their syntactic role.
2 **Picture aiders** (PAs) correspond roughly to adjectives. Their role is to modify the picture we have of an entity.
3 **ACTs** are the basic conceptual actions. Their nearest linguistic equivalents are verbs.
4 **Action Aiders** (AAs) modify the conception of an action, roughly like adverbs.

The other syntactic categories are not encountered as nodes in a CD graph, as their linguistic role is to assist in structuring a sentence rather than adding content. In the CD, structure is indicated by the various arcs connecting the nodes, as illustrated in Fig. 7.1.

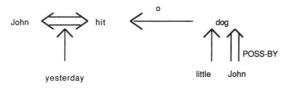

Fig. 7.1 Example CD graph.

The different types of arc used in Fig. 7.1 represent different types of *dependency* between the nodes.

  represents a two-way dependency between items of comparable status, in this case a PP and an ACT.

  represents objective dependency. In this case 'dog' is the object of the action of hitting.

  represents attributive dependency, in these cases an AA modifies an ACT and a PA modifies a PP.

  represents prepositional attachment, and the form of relationship implied has to be added explicitly. Other 'prepositional' relationships include LOC, indicating location.

There are more types of arc, showing for example the conceptual **cases**. In addition to the objective case, there are:

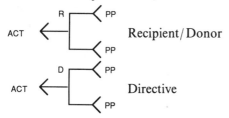

ACT ⟵⟸⟹ Instrumental

Also there are further types of arc showing causation, state change and other relationships.

7.3.1 Semantic primitives

Another feature of CD is that the symbols at the nodes are not words. In our example, the main ACT was rendered as 'hit', but it should really have read 'PROPEL'. PROPEL is one of eleven **semantic primitives**. Others include:

PTRANS – Physical transfer (of location), e.g. 'walk', 'drive'.

ATRANS – Abstract transfer (of possession), e.g. 'buy', 'give'.

MTRANS – Transfer of mental information, e.g. 'tell', 'notify'.

MBUILD – Build a mental representation, e.g. 'decide', 'conclude'.

and also INGEST, EXPEL, MOVE, GRASP, SPEAK, ATTEND.

With such a restricted vocabulary of ACTs, many simple sentences need complex CDs. For example, one involving 'kick' would need to show that in addition to the basic PROPEL action, a PTRANS of a foot POSS-BY the actor was the instrument of the action. This additional information would distinguish 'kick' from the more general 'move', as well as from alternatives such as 'throw' or 'post'. Figure 7.2 shows a CD representation for 'john kicked his ball to bill'.

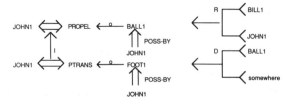

Fig. 7.2 CD for 'john kicked his ball to bill'.

An advantage of using primitives is that there is only one way to record a particular action, as there are no lexical choices within CD. The primitive units in such a system have to be mutually exclusive and cover all that can be said.

Having such a representation makes it possible for us to tell the understander a proposition using one set of words, and to later query it about the same proposition using others.

For example, if we tell an understander that:

John bought a painting from a dealer for 500 pounds.

we should expect the same understander to be able to answer any of the following questions:

How much did the dealer get for the painting?
What did john spend on the picture?

What did john's picture cost him?

What did john get for his 500 pounds?

Examples of 'comprehension' like these show that we are capable of recognizing many different descriptions of the same event as equivalent. They also show that in understanding an apparently simple proposition, we are able to make many inferences about the minute details of the event. We know automatically that in addition to an exchange (ATRANS) of the ownership of the painting, there was an exchange in the opposite direction of money. We are also capable of making a great many other assumptions about the circumstances; inferences which are probably true, unless we know specific information to the contrary. For example, we would normally infer that before the transaction, the dealer was legally the owner of the painting, that in addition to the transfer of ownership, there was probably also a physical transfer of location of the painting. Most likely, it would be PTRANSed to John's home, since if it weren't we might have been told, 'John bought a 500 pound picture for his office' or '... He asked for it to be delivered to his bank.'.

Entirely within CD notation, we could record the sense of 'buy' as implying not one action but at least four, the ATRANSes of the picture and the money, and their corresponding PTRANSes as well. However, having such large representations for every word in the dictionary means a great deal of redundancy and also a very large amount of inferencing at the time the text is read. Schank and Abelson (1977) proposed that understanding requires not only a conceptual memory, but also higher-level memory structures as well. These were known as **scripts** and have been compared with frames as discussed in Chapter 3. The basic idea is that scripts contain sequences of typical events organized around particular human activities. Examples much discussed in the Yale school's writings are the shopping and restaurant scripts. The latter would include components such as:

Being shown to the table,
reading the menu,
ordering,
waiting for the meal,
having the food brought by the waiter,
eating it,
receiving the bill,
paying, leaving.

Each of the components would naturally be encoded in CD notation. A script also includes a 'declaration' of script variables, known as **roles**. In the example script, the roles include $DINER, $WAITER, $MEAL and $CASHIER (possibly more in fancier restaurants). Example events from the above script could be encoded as:

(PTRANS (ACTOR $WAITER) (OBJECT $MEAL) (TO $DINER))

and

(INGEST (ACTOR $DINER) (OBJECT $MEAL))

in a linearized version of the CD graph. On reading a story such as:

John went to a restaurant. The waiter came to him.
He ordered lobster. When the check came, John paid
it and left a large tip. John left the restaurant.

It is possible to answer the question, 'What did John eat?' although that was not explicitly stated. The comprehension process is seen as **script instantiation**, where the understander attempts to find a value for each of the script variables or roles. Just as in Prolog unification, once a script variable has been instantiated, all its occurrences receive the same value. In this way, scripts enable plausible inferences to be made. They also make it possible to solve problems such as reference resolution without using any additional techniques. In the third sentence of the above story, the pronoun 'He' appears as the subject. Any understanding of the text requires that we determine who the referent of the pronoun is. In the text, there are two possible anphoric antecedents, 'John' and 'the waiter'. There are syntactic rules which will work for resolving some but not all of such cases. (We could, for instance, prefer the most recently mentioned noun phrase, which is 'Him', but we have to resolve that one too.) Using scripts, the problem almost disappears, since when the script is instantiated, the role of DINER will be bound to the person who was the logical subject of the sentence which matched the first event in the script, i.e. 'John'. When we come to the point in the script where DINER MTRANSes his order to WAITER, we already have a binding for DINER, and so pronoun references can be resolved without employing any special procedures.

A program called 'SAM', was implemented at Yale, based on this theory, and was interfaced to other programs to produce demonstrations of comprehension. These demonstrations included answering questions that required inferences to be made, paraphrasing whole stories to give not only brief summaries, but also longer versions that were more explicit than the original, and translating into other languages.

7.3.2 Scripts and plans

Schank and Abelson (1977) noted that while scripts could enable common-sense inferencing in understanding to be implemented for stereotyped situations, they couldn't account for all kinds of purposive human action as relayed in stories. In particular, they fail to capture aspects of human motivation and planning that occur in different contexts (or scripts). For example, consider the story text:

Willa was hungry. She picked up the Michelin Guide. She got into her car.

To make the second sentence intelligible, we need to see it as part of a **plan** to achieve the **goal** of alleviating hunger by first finding a restaurant. The whole sequence of actions cannot be considered to be part of a single script unless the notion is to become hopelessly ill-defined. Hence plans are considered to be another high-level memory structure called into play in more novel circumstances than scripts. Interesting stories will include the consideration of conflicting plans and their resolution.

A program called 'PAM' (Plan Applier Mechanism) was constructed by Wilensky to model the way in which stories can be understood by interpreting the underlying goals and plans of the characters in them.

More recently, Schank and his associates have come to consider additional high-level memory structures that appear to play a part in in-depth understanding. These additional structures include themes and plots, and they figure in the explanation of how such cognitive processes as reminding and learning take place. The ideas are presented in Schank (1982) and a program implementing them is described in Dyer (1983).

7.4 SEMANTICS IN LOGIC GRAMMARS

In Chapter 6, the attraction of implementing natural language understanding systems in Prolog was that the DCG notation allowed grammar rules to be represented declaratively, and the Prolog proof procedure could be used as the sole procedural mechanism. A further benefit conferred by Prolog is that the language can be used directly as a semantic representation formalism, obviating the need for any special-purpose notation such as Schank's.

To date, logic grammars have not been concerned with the same sort of everyday understanding that Conceptual Dependency has addressed, but with more directly practical applications such as database query. Some aspects of semantic representation are greatly simplified by restriction to this application domain, particularly by identifying the meaning of words directly with database relations and attributes. This is the case with most common nouns and verbs, which although they belong to distinct syntactic classes, are both logically considered to be predicates. However, such interfaces must also represent the meaning of classes of words that are part of the general non-specialist vocabulary, particularly articles and conjunctions, which play a major role in the logical structure of sentences.

The meaning of the sentence

Some mammals fly.

can be represented logically by the expression

X [mammal (X) & fly (X)],

or slightly adapted for Prolog notation:

exists (X, mammal (X) & fly (X)).

A general semantic interpretation rule for 'some' and 'a' will output expressions of the form

exists (X, R & S)

where X represents the bound variable, R represents a predication over X derived from the subject of the sentence, and S is a predication derived from the verb. Further rules can be defined for other quantifying expressions such as *no, every, all, the, which, how many* and numerals. Such rules are listed in several published accounts of DCG database interfaces, some of which are referred to in Chapter 8. Note that the examples above include expressions which are not included in the Horn clause subset of logic. The standard Prolog proof procedure needs to be augmented to process assertions and queries expressed in such a notation, but that is a minor undertaking.

7.5   INTEGRATING SEMANTICS WITH SYNTAX

So far, our discussion of semantics has been consistent with the multi-level linguistic processing model of Fig. 6.2. We now turn to an examination of approaches to natural language that either attempt to blur the distinction between the syntactic and semantic levels of processing, or else deliberately integrate them closely.

7.5.1   Conceptual parsing implemented

The earlier series of programs constructed by various graduate students at Yale, included a CD parser (ELI for 'English Language Interpreter'), SAM and PAM, and programs for question answering, summarizing and generation in various languages. Several of these programs are described in

Schank and Riesbeck (1981). Following the discussion of each of the programs there, a listing of a simplified version of the program (in Lisp) is presented and discussed.

We could say that the key to Schank's approach is that it is knowledge-based. One type of knowledge accessed in these programs is script knowledge, whose representation we have already discussed. Another source of knowledge, used in the initial language analysis that precedes script application, is the dictionary, but that is a component that all language parsers must have. It can be argued that any approach to parsing could be used for this preliminary analysis; for example, there is no reason why a DCG could not be adapted to output CD representations for individual sentences. However, in a book on knowledge-based systems, it is also worth exploring

```
                          /* Dictionary for McELI.Pro */

dict(jack,[[assign([[cd_form,get_token([person],jack)]])]]).

dict(kite,[[assign([[part_of_speech,noun],
                    [cd_form,[kite]]
                    
                    ])
           
           ]]).

dict(start,[[assign([[part_of_speech,_],
                     [cd_form,nil]]),
             next_packet([[test(part_of_speech,noun_phrase),
                          assign([[subject,@cd_form]]),
                          next_packet([[test(part_of_speech,verb),
                                       assign([[concept,@cd_form]])
                                       ]])
                          
                          ]])
            ]]).

dict(got,[[assign([[part_of_speech,verb],
                   [cd_form,[atrans,[actor,get_var1],
                                    [object,get_var2],
                                    [to,get_var1],
                                    [from,get_var3]]
                    ],
                    [get_var1,@subject],
                    [get_var2,nil],
                    [get_var3,nil]]),
           next_packet([[test(part_of_speech,noun_phrase),
                        assign([[get_var2,@cd_form]])
                        ]])
          ]]).

dict(a,[[test(part_of_speech,noun),
         assign([[get_var2,@cd_form]])
         ]]
        ]]).
```

Fig. 7.3 Dictionary entries for McELI in Prolog notation.

the way in which the ELI parser has been constructed as a production system.

The dictionary entries correspond roughly to the individual production rules in any other production system. Each entry comprises the name of the word and its **packet**. The packet is a list of **requests**, each of which is a list of up to three of the following items: test (List of tests), assign (List of assignments), next packet (Packet), each occurring only once. Each individual request in the packet represents one sense for the word. Within the request, the **test**, if present, corresponds to the condition in a production rule, and the **assign** and **next-packet** components correspond to actions and sub-goals respectively. Such subgoals would be found among the conditions in a conventional production rule, whereas here they are applied after any assignments are made, so the control regime cannot be compared directly with that of an expert system.

Figure 7.3 illustrates some dictionary entries from a simplified version of ELI, based on the didactic version McELI, described in Schank and Riesbeck (1981). The syntax in which they are expressed has been adapted to Prolog notation. The word senses shown are sufficient to allow the program to produce the CD representation for the sentence

jack got a kite.

In its operating cycle, the parser loads the dictionary entry for the next word on to its evaluation stack, and then seeks to apply the tests and actions in the entries on the stack. The CD that constitutes the output of the analysis is produced by filling in a template that appears within the request associated with the main verb of the sentence. By contrast, the dictionary entries for nouns can be said to play a more passive role in the processing. The parsing strategy depends on the strong *expectations* that verb entries have about the noun phrases that can fill their case roles. As the verb does not come first in English, the analysis has to begin before the verb's entry is available, and so a special word, *start, is prepended to the input list of words. It has the basic expectation that the main sentence is structured into a noun phrase and verb. The individual verbs have their own expectations, depending on their transitivity, about the objects or complements that may follow.

7.5.2 Dypar

A more recent parser was constructed by Dyer (1983), based on a different control structure, which does not stack the dictionary packets so that they are processed in a predetermined order. Instead, each word is represented by a distinct process known as a **demon**. A demon remains alive so long as it has some test whose result is not yet evaluated. Values for slots in verbal case frames are established by spawning further demons. Expectations such as these may not be satisfied immediately or at all, and so the demon is an autonomous process which may remain alive for an indeterminate time.

To implement this pseudo-concurrency, each demon has an activation record which is examined during each processing cycle to see if its tests can be satisfied or the demon can be killed in the light of the new state of the working memory. The main loop of McDYPAR is thus to carry out 'word tasks' and then 'demon tasks'. The former means to load the word from the dictionary and to spawn any associated demons, and the latter is concerned with updating the active demons.

Formally, there is no limit to the sort of process which may be implemented by a demon, and so in the BORIS system of which DYPAR is a component, the higher-level reasoning has been implemented along with the purely linguistic processing in a unified system. One of the main motivations for the control structure chosen is psychological. From this point of view, the linguistic model of language processing separated into analytically distinct levels as suggested by Fig. 6.2 is implausible. In practice, each level of processing interacts with those above and below, and this interchange of information much reduces the nondeterminism in the analysis process. DYPAR is not the only natural language system that adopts such a control strategy: the HEARSAY speech understanding system uses what is termed a 'blackboard' to maintain an agenda of processes dealing with several different levels of analysis. Chapter 9 of Hayes-Roth *et al.* (1983) gives an overview.

7.5.3 Conceptual parsing and linguistics

Both ELI and DYPAR adopt an apparently bottom-up approach, having no unified representation of English grammar at all. This apparent omission of syntax was foreshadowed in this quotation from Schank's early introduction to the Conceptual Dependency theory:

'Whereas no-one would claim today that syntactic analysis of a sentence is sufficient for programs which use natural language, it may not even be necessary.'

This statement has led many linguistics to ridicule the approach, but it is in fact very far from true that the programs ignore syntax. The syntactic facts of the language are present in the program's knowledge base, but rather than being collected together in a set of syntactic rules, they are distributed throughout the dictionary of information about individual words. The dictionary entries for verbs, for example, contain expectations about the conceptual categories of the nouns that may fill their various case roles, and use is made of information that can be deduced from word order and from the choices of auxiliaries and prepositions.

7.6 INCREMENTAL SEMANTIC ANALYSIS IN LOGIC GRAMMARS

A psychological motivation for integrating the processing on the different linguistic levels has been introduced, and certainly there is no reason why logic grammars cannot also be used to implement psychologically motivated language understanding systems. There are, however, also some practical reasons for not carrying out semantic interpretation only on completely parsed sentences:

- Lexical subcategorization knowledge can be used in disambiguation. If this is done during the parse, it can help eliminate potential structural ambiguities as well as those arising out of word senses alone.
- A parser that has successfully recognized a component of a sentence, but fails in analysing another, will be better able to provide error recovery if it has a semantic analysis of the good component.

Some aspects of semantic interpretation, particularly the resolution of the various ambiguities introduced at the beginning of the chapter, are not processes that operate at the sentence level. The information needed may not be fully available until the analysis of a later sentence has already begun. For example, in the sentence pair that illustrated the sense ambiguity of 'bank' and reference ambiguity of 'it', the most likely interpretation of 'bank' after reading only the first sentence was the financial one, but after the second sentence, the river bank sense seemed more appropriate. This shows that a semantic interpretation system should be prepared to change its representation in the light of new information that may not arise in the same sentence.

Mellish (1985) describes a program that analysed descriptive noun phrases used to specify mechanics problems. In addition to simple reference resolution as described above, this program had to determine the cardinality of the sets denoted by plural noun phrases, and the mappings between members of sets where relationships are described. These problems are illustrated in the following short texts:

Some particles are free to move on a smooth table. The particles have mass b and c.

The particles are attached to the strings.

In the first text, the cardinality of the set of particles is not known until the second sentence is analysed. The latter is not straightforward, since it involves establishing that the 'has mass' predicate relates all of the members of the set of particles denoted by the subject of that sentence to b and c, and that both noun phrases involving particles refer to the same set. In the second text, there is uncertainty over whether each particle is connected to only one, a subset, or all of the strings.

Mellish argues that to accomodate all of these difficulties of interpretation, it is necessary to use a semantic representation that can record incomplete information which is updated after taking account of subsequent text.

At the theoretical level, this means a representation is needed that is **intensional** in that the objects in it are not the real-world objects denoted by noun phrases, but the conceptual objects evoked by the descriptions, called by Mellish 'reference entities'. Ultimately, the goal of semantic analysis is to build a model of the real-world objects and their relationships, but intermediate levels of semantic analysis are required that deal in reference entities. During processing, there may be more than one reference entity that corresponds to a single real-world entity, until co-reference is established.

At the practical level, the updatable semantic representation is implemented using assertions in the Prolog database, made by semantic routines at the time they are called by the corresponding syntactic phrase rules. In contrast to what we might call the standard DCG approach, the semantic representation is not built up as a single structure argument to the *sentence* goal.

In conclusion, Mellish's approach has demonstrated the feasibility of using incremental semantic interpretation, and both this work and that of Schank have demonstrated that much of semantics operates independently of the boundaries of individual sentences.

SUMMARY
Chapter 7

The goal of semantics in natural language is to produce a representation of the logical propositions underlying a text (its sense) in such a way that the individuals and objects are differentiated correctly (reference).

In determining sense and reference, a natural language understander must be able to resolve ambiguities of reference, structure, quantifier scope and word sense.

It is also necessary to map paraphrases into the same meaning representation, so that the correct inferences may be made from a text.

In order to account for the inferences made in comprehending simple stories, complex high-level memory structures seem to be necessary. Some of these models of memory have been developed at Yale by Schank and his students.

Using a script-based approach to natural language analysis, some of the disambiguation problems referred to above are easily resolved. However, scripts do not solve all the problems of natural language understanding and other more dynamic memory structures are required.

In analysing stories, problems of accurately representing quantifiers and their relative scope do not arise. These problems have been tackled in Logic grammars that have been developed for more practical applications.

Although syntax and semantics are analytically distinct, there are good reasons, both psychological and practical, for both levels of procesing to be closely integrated.

Programs have been developed within both the CD and DCG frameworks that integrate syntax and semantics closely in parsing.

**EXERCISES
AND PROJECTS
Chapter 7**

E7.1 Draw the two parses for the ambiguous sentence: 'Allies push bottles up German rear'.

E7.2 Make a collection of texts including anaphoric pronouns, and write down the knowledge required to disambiguate them. Estimate the proportion that can be dealt with directly by lexical subcategorization.

E7.3 Draw a Conceptual Dependency Graph for the sentence: Tim concluded that Dora had stabbed herself'.

E7.4 Decide what events should go into scripts for going on holiday and applying for a job.

E7.5 Collect or invent stories, like the example involving Willa's hunger, that need to be explained in terms of plans. Referring to a planning program such as WARPLAN (see Chapter 5), attempt to describe the steps in the plan rigorously.

E7.6 Expand the dictionary of McELI.Pro so that it will have the definitions needed to parse other sentences from the shopping script.

E7.7 Adapt a DCG grammar such as that published in Pereira and Warren (see Chapter 6) so that it outputs CD structures.

8

INTELLIGENT INTERFACES
TO COMPUTER SYSTEMS

The aim of this chapter is to show how the techniques of IKBS introduced to date can be applied to make other computer systems easier to use. We start by reviewing the direct application of expert system and ICAI techniques to the human–computer interface. We then turn to the most frequent application area for natural language interfaces, that of access to databases by naïve end users. In that context, we consider the important design issue of whether the interface should be specialized to the application domain or should be portable. We then look at potential applications of natural language, planning and expert system techniques together in the context of rich computing environments such as operating systems.

8.1 INTELLIGENT FRONT ENDS

In Chapters 1 and 5, we have encountered two applications of the intelligent knowledge-based approach: expert systems providing advice on problems in limited specialized domains, and intelligent computer-aided instruction and tutoring. The effective use of computer software often requires considerable expertise depending on the application. It is therefore appropriate to consider whether similar knowledge-based approaches can help users exploit a computer package to solve a particular problem. Computer systems software and application packages can thus become the problem domain for IKBS.

Such an advisor can be built using IKBS techniques and software as a standalone system, where the user has to leave what he is doing with the package and turn to the separate expert system for advice. Where, on the other hand, the computer-based expert or tutor is closely coupled to the application package, we refer to it as an 'Intelligent Front End' or 'IFE'. As with other terms used in IKBS, 'IFE' means different things to different people.

There are two reasons why a user may experience difficulty in using a computer package effectively:

1 A lack of knowledge of the language or interaction protocol through which the package's functions may be invoked. For example, in using a statistics package, an expert statistician who wants to apply a T-test to a set of data may simply not know the command to select a T-test or the syntax in which parameters are supplied and options selected.

2 The user may not only lack the knowledge of the language of the package, but may also be ignorant of its underlying concepts. For example, a user of the statistics package may have some medical, social or psychological data to be analysed, but be unaware of which statistical tests should be used to test his hypothesis. (Strictly, this matter should be considered before any data are collected, when the experiment or survey is being designed.)

The former problem, it can be argued, is not one that merits the IKBS approach, but is simply one of effective human–computer interaction (HCI). The solution to this problem is to provide either a better user interface within the applications itself, perhaps with more prompting through menus, forms and on-line help text, or else better user training and documentation. The proper time and place to attend to HCI is within the analysis and design of the application package, when HCI should be given the same consideration as functional requirements in the specification and design phases. A separate interface created *post hoc* is an inferior alternative requiring more effort in analysis and in system integration – 'sticking plaster' in the words of Prof. Tom Addis.

Nevertheless, if such a bolt-on interface is to be built simply to remedy HCI deficiencies, IKBS techniques may well be appropriate. In particular, natural language interfaces, to which we return below, have often addressed this problem by removing the need for a user to learn the command language of a particular product.

8.1.1 Examples of intelligent front-ends

Bundy (1984) reviews several examples of intelligent front ends that address problem 2, that of supporting user problem solving with a computer package. He also gives an overview of the knowledge requirements of an intelligent front end and its software architecture. Among the surveyed systems are:

• SACON, which advises on the use of a finite element package for structural analysis.

- ECO, which assists in building ecological simulation models in Fortran.
- ASA, a statistical advisor, which is designed to help a psychologist select and then apply an appropriate statistical test to experiment data.

8.1.2   Dialogue with an expert IFE

An interface to another computer system embodies knowledge about the tasks that can be carried out within the object system called 'task specification knowledge' and also a description of the object system's commands and their relationships with the tasks. Finally, it must have a means of translating from its own input formats to a task specification.

In a front end that is not constructed with IKBS techniques, this knowledge can be entirely procedural. Such a program branches to subcomponents that build up object system commands according to choices made by the user who has had the benefit of displayed advisory text and a detailed questionnaire driven by the interface to clarify requirements. Interfaces like this can be readily built in conventional programming languages, if the package functions can be accessed as external subroutines (or failing that, by implementing the interface as a **pseudo-terminal** in a UNIX-like environment).

As always, the distinctive feature of the IKBS approach is to encode the knowledge declaratively. Only in this way is it possible to make the interface as flexible as possible, providing for a mixed-initiative dialogue (as exemplified in SCHOLAR, described in Chapter 5), and to provide the usual IKBS justification and explanation facilities. Attempts have been made to use standard expert system shells such as EMYCIN (in SACON for example). However, such software does not have the representation structure both to represent the task specification declaratively and to translate from the interface's own language to that of the package.

AI techniques other than rule-based representation, for example planning, may be required where the input required by the object system is complex. A feature that some IFEs provide is user-adaptability, where either the system automatically builds a model of the user on the basis of his monitored responses, or else the user explicitly requests a more-or-less helpful mode of dialogue. Again, expert system shells are not designed specifically to support such dialogues.

8.2   NATURAL-LANGUAGE INTERFACES

The aim of a natural-language interface to an existing software product is to allow the latter to be used by a 'naïve end user' who does not know its command language. In principle, the software product could be anything from a specific application, such as an in-house data processing system to a general-purpose programming language. It is not cost-effective to develop natural-language interfaces to the former, since the development effort will not be 'repaid' by re-use with other applications. There have been attempts at applying natural-language input to program construction, but the real problems in program development lie in getting the data and control structures right rather than in the superficial linguistic forms in which they are expressed. Somewhere between these two extremes lie general-purpose software items that are invoked by commands extending to one or two lines rather than the hundreds of lines in programs. Such packages include operating system utilities, database query languages, bibliographic retrieval systems, statistics packages, and more recently expert systems. We shall consider some of these later, after the most popular application for natural language interface techniques, database queries.

8.2.1   Database query in natural language

The earliest well-publicised natural-language interface to a database was Woods' LUNAR system, dated 1972, which allowed geologists to request information from a database about lunar rock samples obtained in the Apollo explorations. At around the same time, the idea of a database as a program-independent structured collection of data and an organizational resource was being developed and formalized. The structural models underlying databases address the same issues as knowledge representation, and therefore constitute a semantic framework for representing retrieval requests from a database. Accordingly, work on the natural language interface can start from the basis of a given semantics.

8.2.2   Database query languages

There are many different database query languages, each associated with

emp_no	name	department	location	salary
e102	brown	marketing	manchester	22500
e320	whyte	distribut'n	manchester	9050
e330	plum	training	manchester	11250
e340	greene	sales	manchester	27800
e341	black	printing	wapping	14000
e411	gray	public rel	manchester	17000

Fig. 8.1   A sample 'table' in a relational database

either a particular class of database structure or a particular database product within a class. Relational databases are increasingly popular, owing to their transparent organization in terms of simple two-dimensional tables where the columns represent attributes. An example table from a relational database is shown in Fig. 8.1.

A database query can be characterized as a request for a selection of tuples (records) from the database which simultaneously constitute a **row subset** and a **column subset** of a table. (More complex queries are subsets of virtual tables comprising the composition or join of two or more tables.)

The statement of a query must show which attributes, and their corresponding value ranges, are the selection criteria for the row subset. For example, the attributes and values salary > 12000 and location = Manchester will pick out only the first, fourth and sixth rows in the table in Fig. 8.1. The column subset is specified by merely quoting the names of the wanted columns. A typical query language has selected queries expressed in a format such as:

LIST column_names WHERE expression

with expression being a Boolean combination of simple expressions of the form:

column_name operator value

An example query in this language might be

LIST NAME, DEPARTMENT WHERE SALARY > 12000 AND
LOCATION = MANCHESTER

From the table in Fig. 8.1, this would result in the following data being displayed:

NAME	DEPARTMENT
brown	marketing
greene	sales
gray	public rel

8.2.3 Are NL database interfaces needed?

It may seem that the English-like syntax and vocabulary of this query language would be sufficiently straightforward for users to make the natural-language interface superfluous. There are however, scores of similar query languages, and most have slight differences of syntax and use different keywords. For example, where our example has used 'LIST' others have used 'SHOW', 'DISPLAY', 'PRINT', 'SELECT', 'FIND', 'REPORT', and 'FOR', 'WITH', 'HAVING' in place of 'WHERE'. Relational and Boolean operators may differ, with '.GT', FORTRAN-style instead of '>' and 'AND' for '&' or ',' Conjuncts may need to be bracketed and string values enclosed in quotes in some systems. Where a database contains more than one table, the attribute names have to be qualified. In some packages, this is done by a separate command, opening a particular table, in others, each attribute name has to be qualified by the table name (e.g. EMPLOYEE.NAME).

In addition to the whims of the language designer, the database administrator may choose different words for what is conceptually the same entity or attribute. For example, DEPARTMENT may be DEPT, DEPT_ NAME, GROUP, TASK_GROUP, SECTION, or DIVISION; alternatively these names may refer to distinct entities.

8.2.4 Why database query is a popular NLU testbed

As noted earlier, the query as expressed in the database query language can be taken as the semantic representation for the natural-language expression. This frees the researcher or designer to concentrate on other aspects of the analysis process. It is perhaps for this reason that work on the general semantics of natural language is much less advanced than that on syntax and syntactic parsing.

Domain-specific semantic representation is one reason why database applications for natural-language interfaces are more tractable than general natural-language understanding systems. Another is that in addition to the limited range of semantic structures, the vocabulary is clearly delimited in a database system. The program's dictionary need include only the widely used 'function words' of the language, a range of general verbs and nouns that might be used to phrase commands or requests, and words denoting the entities and their attributes in the database. The 'closed world' assumption about databases means that anyone using a natural-language query facility will know the scope of the database, and the kind of questions he can ask about its contents, and will not expect the system to have linguistic competence outside this domain.

We can express this point differently, by saying that a natural-language interface to a database is not really analysing natural language at all. The language it parses is just another formal language that happens to have more structure and vocabulary in common with natural language than does a standard query language. Its success will depend on the extent that it handles synonymy and paraphrase as discussed in Chapter 7.

8.2.5 Examples of natural-language database interfaces

We will now review several representative natural-language query systems, concentrating on the specific issues that each has addressed.

Rendezvous

An early natural language interface developed around 1975 by Codd (the inventor of the relational database model) was named 'RENDEZVOUS'. The reason for this name was its design philosophy which was that its representation of the request behind a query should come to meet that of the user, by whatever means is possible. To begin with, the system tried to analyse the user's input using the English parser, but if that failed, there were several alternative strategies that could be used as a 'fall-back'. If single words were not recognized or were mis-spelled, then the linguistic analysis could resume after a brief clarification dialogue. If, however, the parse failed more seriously, the system could resort to query formulation entirely by a prompt-and-answer dialogue.

The important feature of this system, therefore, was that a useable natural language interface must be designed for robustness, so that it doesn't fail completely if the user types something ungrammatical or otherwise unrecognizable. This design criterion is now taken for granted in any natural language interface that is intended for practical rather than experimental use.

LIFER – semantic grammars and 'human engineering'

Hendrix *et al.* (1978) describe a system and approach to the construction of a natural language interface that concentrates much more on the robustness of its dialogue than on purely linguistic matters. The LIFER system is not a single specialized interface but a system for generating interfaces to particular databases and other applications. The core of the system does not contain any linguistic knowledge, but the application designer defines the language that a LIFER interface is initially capable of recognizing. Since the designer will not normally be a linguistics expert, the grammar is expressed in terms of patterns made up of literal words and variable expressions that are meaningful in the application context rather than abstract linguistic categories like noun and verb. For example, the top level rule in such a grammar may be:

LIFER.TOP.GRAMMAR => <SHOWME> <ATT_LIST>
<EMPLOYEE>

<SHOWME> is marked as a variable by the angled brackets, and in lower-level rules, can be defined to match such alternative expressions as '[Can you [please]] show me', 'List', 'I'd like to see' 'What are' and 'What is'. Similarly, <ATT_LIST> can be expanded to permit alternative ways of expressing a list of attributes whose values are required, and <EMPLOYEE> corresponds to the table and row selection part of a standard query. Attached to each rule in the grammar is a direct translation into the object query language. A grammar using category labels taken direct from the application domain instead of linguistic word and phrase classes has been labelled a 'semantic grammar'.

The interesting features of LIFER are the techniques it uses to enhance the robustness of the dialogue. Clearly, a LIFER grammar writer will not foresee every construction a potential user might employ, and there will be occasions when it will fail to parse some input. LIFER does not give up in these circumstances. At a low level, it can call upon a spelling corrector to see if a word may have been mis-spelled. If that doesn't help, it tries to see if the input is elliptical. This means that it is incomplete but its general pattern resembles the previous input, but with a common phrase omitted. Figure 8.2 shows an example.

```
: Give me the salary and job title of John Fox
PARSED!
(SALARY $35,750 JOB-TITLE systems analyst)

: age and grade
Trying Ellipsis : GIVE ME THE AGE AND GRADE OF JOHN FOX
(AGE 34 GRADE A6)
```

Fig. 8.2   LIFER dialogue showing ellipsis handling.

If after trying ellipsis, the parse has still failed, LIFER reports the context in which the parse failed, and allows the user to extend the grammar by defining the sentence as a paraphrase of another sentence that LIFER can parse. Figure 8.3 shows how this can be done for simple synonyms:

```
: Who in DP is grade B2
Trying Ellipsis. ELLIPSIS HAS FAILED.
THE PARSER DOES NOT EXPECT THE WORD 'DP' TO FOLLOW 'WHO IN'.
Options for next word or meta-symbol are:
<DEPT-NAME> <LOCATION>

: What is a <DEPT-NAME>

<DEPT-NAME> may be any member of the set
    [ACCOUNTS SALES MARKETING SERVICING DISTRIBUTION]

<DEPT-NAME> may be any sequence of words following one of the patterns:
    <DEPT-NAME> => MANAGEMENT SERVICES
                  QUALITY CONTROL
                  CUSTOMER SERVICES

: Define DP like MANAGEMENT SERVICES
PARSED!
DP

: Redo -3
PARSED!
(ID 10234 EMP-NAME Frank Jones)
(ID 01254 EMP-NAME Georgina Brown)
:
```

Fig. 8.3   LIFER paraphrase capabilities.

Paraphrases involving more wholesale re-arrangement of the input can also be handled. For example, the user can say

: Let 'For Mary Baker, list age qualification and start date' be a paraphrase of 'List the age qualification and start date of Mary Baker'

and LIFER will add a new production to its top-level grammar, generalizing the transformation as far as is legitimate.

The main strengths of LIFER are in the robustness of the systems developed with it. This has been termed 'human engineering' by Hendrix, and covers both the exploitation of dialogue to allow elliptical input and the user-adaptability of the system achieved by making its language extensible. The former is an important factor in favour of natural language for habitual users, for whom it is often claimed to be too verbose in comparison with other interaction techniques. The extensibility of the language, however, takes the LIFER approach away from the mainstream of natural language understanding, since users tend to define their own personal artificial languages rather than sticking to 'good English'.

Although Hendrix claims that some new interfaces to specific databases have been constructed with as little as a week's effort, the approach has been heavily criticized for the way its linguistic knowledge does not generalize to other domains. The system makes no use at all of generally known linguistic rules or of dictionary definitions of words used independently of the particular database. As a consequence, each new application starts from the same knowledge-poor base.

8.3 LINGUISTICALLY MOTIVATED INTERFACES

An alternative approach to the development of a natural-language interface is to use a standard grammar of English or whatever language the system recognizes. This means that each new application does not involve re-inventing the whole wheel. At least the grammar used for the initial stage of linguistic processing should be common, even if a large part of the dictionary has to be rewritten to port the interface to a new domain.

8.3.1 Database interfaces using DCG notation

Typical of the more linguistically motivated approaches have been the experimental database interfaces constructed in Prolog using the DCG. These include the work of Dahl (1982), McCord (1982) and Warren and Pereira (1982) – the system developed by the latter known as 'CHAT-80'. These systems can process more sophisticated grammatical structures than systems like LIFER. For example, CHAT-80 can parse the query: 'Which are the continents no country in which contains more than two cities whose population exceeds 1 million?'.

Typically, the DCG-based systems have exploited other features of Prolog besides the grammar-rule notation. In Dahl's program, the query is translated not into a syntactic parse tree like those shown in Chapter 6, but directly into a formal logical representation. McCord's program and CHAT-80 both have a modular structure building up logic queries in three phases. In CHAT-80, these are syntactic parsing, semantic interpretation and finally quantifier scoping. In all three programs the rules for all of these structure-building operations are expressed declaratively in Prolog. The object database in each program is also implemented as a set of Prolog clauses.

The semantic representation of a query is a logical formula, not restricted to the Horn clause subset. Formulae involving explicit existential quantifiers can be constructed by the semantic routines and interpreted by the query evaluator. Since many database queries involve numerical quantifiers as well as the basic first-order predicate logic quantifiers, McCord's program was capable of handling numeric quantifiers – num (N):, atleast (N):, almost (N): – and several others.

8.3.2 Portability in database interfaces

The DCG-based programs have demonstrated the feasibility of linguistically sophisticated interfaces to databases. Such interfaces embody the general rules of language syntax and of semantic interpretation for the important classes of words in the domain-independent lexicon, and do not require *ad hoc* grammars to be constructed afresh for each new database. In systems that are interfaced to external databases rather than Prolog simulations, this feature is also desirable.

'Second-generation' database interface architectures are modular, separating this general linguistic knowledge from domain-specific knowledge that has to be provided for each new application, keeping the latter to a minimum. This is the basic philosophy of the system developed by Boguraev and Sparck-Jones (1982). Altogether, their system applies four stages of analysis and translation to an English question, each producing a different structured representation for the query: The analyser, using knowledge of linguistic syntax and semantics, produces a meaning representation. A logic representation is produced from that by an 'extractor' whose knowledge base describes the relationship between linguistic and logical structures. A translator builds a query representation from the logic representation using domain world knowledge, and finally, a database search specification is built using a convertor that uses knowledge of the database organization. Only the last two components make any use of database-specific knowledge.

At the same time, a modular interface should ideally retain as much as possible of the dialogue handling capability and 'human engineering' features of the LIFER approach. The architecture proposed by Konolige (1979) is designed to provide a LIFER-like human interface, incorporating a much more sophisticated and modular language analysis component.

Commercial natural language database interfaces

The technology of database interfacing in natural language is now sufficiently mature for it to be feasible to provide such interfaces or tools to build them on a commercial basis. A recent review in the journal *Expert Systems User* was able to list six such products available to access a variety of database systems on both mainframe and personal computers.

8.4 NON-DATABASE INTERFACES

Recently, natural-language interfaces have been built to classes of software other than databases. For example, expert systems developed at Stanford Research Institute, where LIFER originated, have been given simple natural language interfaces using semantic grammars. An important use for the natural-language interface in an expert system is to provide for the 'mixed initiative' style of dialogue that enables the user to request run-time explanation and justification without requiring a knowledge of commands.

A natural-language interface to the XSEL expert system (mentioned in conjunction with XCON in Chapter 1) is being developed at Carnegie-Mellon University by Carbonell and associates.

Perhaps more interesting are the efforts to provide natural-language interfaces to operating systems and other rich computing environments. Hayes and Carbonell (1983) discuss some of the opportunities that a sophisticated interface could provide to help users undo their mistakes, for example in the following dialogue extracts:

USER:	Print mainmenu. rel on the line printer.
SYSTEM:	MAINMENU. REL is not a printable file.
USER:	Oops, I meant mainmenu.cob.
USER:	Move report.txt to the backup directory.
SYSTEM:	REPORT.TXT inserted in the backup, and removed from the current directory.
USER:	I meant copy not move.
USER:	Is mainmenu.cob being printed yet?
SYSTEM:	The printer is offline and mainmenu.cob is 25th in the queue.
USER:	Forget it then.

In these cases, the natural language system has to be endowed with knowledge of the pragmatics of language use as well as semantic subcategorization to resolve anaphoric references to previous requests rather than objects. The first two examples are of ellipsis, which can be recovered using the same way as LIFER does in the database context. However, what is interesting in this context is what happens after the ellipsis has been recovered. In the first example, the original request failed simply because the argument wasn't an appropriate type of object for the desired operation. In the second example, however, the user's original request was carried out. The correction implies that the original operation should be undone and replaced with the revised request (or some further operation such as a re-copy from the backup to the original directory applied so that the desired goal-state will be reached). Here the pragmatic meaning of the user's declarative sentence is not that a fact is being a volunteered, but that a new command is being given.

Some conventional job-control languages provide an approximation to some of these facilities, but without the flexibility provided by natural language input, the user must learn not only the JCL commands for the various requests, but also the restrictions placed on the ellipsis.

In the last interaction, we have a nice example of an anaphoric pronoun, 'it', that is not used to refer to an object in the preceding discourse, but to a previous command. However, it is not the most recent command that is being referred to, but one whose result is the topic of the previous question. This again requires inferences to be made concerning the underlying operations and their effects. Further, the sense of 'forget' that is intended here is not directly related to the word's propositional meaning, but can only be interpreted as having pragmatic meaning.

An intelligent front end to an operating system should be able to provide help in accessing system functions and explanations for error messages, as well as providing a direct means of giving instructions to the system. Such advice-giving is the main role for UC – the 'UNIX Consultant' (Wilensky, 1984). In this system, the user might input a question such as:

Why can't I remove the directory tmp?

and receive an answer such as:

The directory tmp must be empty before the directory can be removed.

UC is also able to answer questions where the user asks about a specific problem, producing a generalized solution. UC has several significant features:

1 It can handle idiomatic English (and Spanish), since its linguistic knowledge-base includes information about whole phrases that should be treated as units rather than being analysed during parsing.
2 It has a sophisticated language generation component, whereas some of the database interfaces we have described simply present the retrieved information as formatted by the DBMS.

3   An important design feature of UC is that its linguistic response generator, PHRED (Jacobs 1985), and parser, PHRAN, both use the same declarative knowledge base of language patterns.

4   It has a direct interface to the operating system, so that it can find out information about the current state of entities in the query (e.g. tmp).

8.5   INTEGRATING NATURAL LANGUAGE WITH OTHER IKBS TECHNIQUES

Most of the interfaces reviewed above have inference capabilities in addition to the language parser. A more complete marriage of natural language analysis and generation with expert systems or planners will provide flexible easy-to-use intelligent front ends that can benefit a wide range of users in all application areas. On the one hand, standard expert system shells are seen as being in need of a much better user interface, and on the other hand natural language interfaces need to use real-world knowledge to solve both semantic analysis and domain reasoning problems. We single out two of the aforementioned interfaces for further comment.

CHAT-80 uses information about the sizes of the different database tables in order to produce an optimal query-processing strategy, after the natural language analysis has been completed. In testing an earlier version, it had been found that in comparison with the parsing and semantic interpretation phases, query evaluation in the Prolog database was relatively slow, producing unacceptable overall response times.

UC does not rely simply on pre-stored associations with anticipated queries and the corresponding operating system commands or messages, but instead, derives a **plan** to achieve the user's goal, using a deductive model of the operating system's commands and their effect on the filestore and its components.

SUMMARY
Chapter 8

An important class of application for IKBS techniques is the provision of intelligent interfaces to other computer systems.

Where the user's basic understanding of the application requires knowledge-based support, such an intelligent front-end will resemble an expert system. However, in addition to the domain knowledge-base, the IFE requires knowledge of the application package's command language. Typical expert system shells are not designed to represent the syntax of a language nor do their control structures support the management of an interface.

A second strand of IKBS techniques for providing user-friendly interfaces is natural-language understanding.

In the constrained domain of a computer package, semantic interpretation can be reduced to translation of natural language input to the command language of the package. This simplification allows natural-language interfaces to give more impressive performance than the state of the art in general semantic theory would suggest is possible.

The most popular application to date for applied natural-language interfaces is in the processing of database queries. Many systems have been constructed in research laboratories, and there are at least half a dozen commercial products for this application.

Natural-language interfaces can provide additional benefits when they use dialogue context to interpret elliptical user input.

Recently, much work in natural-language interfacing has been accomplished within the DCG framework, exploiting Prolog's ability to represent and manipulate semantic representations as well as to parse directly from grammars written in grammar-rule notation.

Richer computing environments, such as operating systems, have been increasingly popular applications for more sophisticated natural-language interfaces.

Natural-language interfaces use additional inferential techniques to apply various kinds of real-world knowledge in addition to purely linguistic rules.

EXCERCISES AND PROJECTS Chapter 8

E8.1 Design an interactive program using an IKBS approach to provide help on using a statistical package such as SPSS or MINITAB. The program should establish the user' requirements in an interactive dialogue and produce a file of commands for the package.

E8.2 Collect or contrive a sample series of related database queries involving the kind of ellipsis that LIFER can handle, and establish how they would need to be entered using conventional database query languages. Do a keystroke analysis to see if the LIFER approach requires the user to type more or less to enter the series of queries.

E8.3 Design a program that will interactively augment the rules of a DGC-based parser in the same way that LIFER does.

E8.4 Develop a suitable dictionary for a published database interface like McCord (1982) applied to a database of your own.

E8.5 Establish whether the approach of McCord (1982) can be adapted to incorporate the error recovery, ellipsis and pragmatic features of the work of Hendrix and of Hayes and Carbonell.

9

FURTHER READING

The IKBS and artificial intelligence research community is extensive, and consequently its research literature is voluminous. Nevertheless, the number of introductory texts is still small, and there are very few that address the applications as opposed to the basic techniques of the subject, on which there are some good texts.

After the present introduction to what IKBS is, I hope the reader will be interested in finding more about how it is done. Winston (1984) and its companion volume Winston and Horn (1981) are well established texts on the basic methods of AI and their implementation in Lisp. Charniak and McDermott (1985) is a more recent alternative, covering in detail the techniques needed to implement the applications described here, although again using Lisp as the vehicle. Readers preferring to stay with Prolog, the language used for illustrations in this book, may prefer Bratko (1986).

To broaden awareness of the range of past research in AI and its applications, Barr and Feigenbaum (1982) is an invaluable reference work. To keep abreast of new developments is more difficult, as the number of journals and conference series dealing with IKBS and AI is mushrooming. The major journal in AI is *Artificial Intelligence*, but recent new titles are the *Journal of Automated Reasoning, Data and Knowledge Engineering*, and *AI Magazine*. Expert systems work is also reported in many other journals, including the *Communications of the Association for Computing Machinery (CACM), International Journal of Man-Machine Studies (IJMMS), New Generation Computing, Information Technology: Research and Development, Journal of Information Technology, Communications of the ACM*, and several of the IEEE Computing publications. CACM (September 1985) and IJMMS (1984) have run special issues on knowledge engineering and expert systems respectively. Several of the IJMMS papers have been collected together in book form as Coombs (1984).

The major AI conference is the biennial International Joint Conference on

Artificial Intelligence (IJCAI), but other significant series are the annual conference of the American Association for Artificial Intelligence (AAAI), the European Conference on Artificial Intelligence (ECAI) and the conference of the Society for the Study of Artificial Intelligence and the Simulation of Behaviour (AISB), the last two taking place in alternating years in Europe. More recent conference series include several on expert systems including the annual conference of the BCS Expert Systems Group, two separate conference series on logic programming and several on natural language understanding, many under the auspices of the Association for Computational Linguistics. All of the conferences listed above publish full preceedings of papers presented.

Alvey News is the newsletter of the Alvey programme of research and development, and contains progress reports on projects sponsored by the programme. Work under the European ESPRIT programme is reported in the annual ESPRIT Technical Week, whose proceedings are also published.

CHAPTER 1

The best way to proceed after reading Chapter 1 is to obtain a detailed knowledge of one major expert system, its capabilities and its operation. Such an understanding of MYCIN can be obtained from either Shortliffe (1976) or Cendrowska and Bramer (1984). Alty and Coombs (1984) contains descriptions of eight early expert systems in the research literature. The different approaches that can be used to construct an expert system, and knowledge of some of the software tools available, are considered in Hayes-Roth *et al.* (1983). Clancey (1983) and Kidd (1985) both discuss aspects of human–machine interaction with expert systems, Clancey discussing the knowledge structures needed to support adequate explanation, and Kidd discussing the need for the system to support the problem-solving strategy used by the human expert.

CHAPTER 2

Clocksin and Mellish (1984) is the original text on Prolog, and has defined the *de facto* standard for later implementations of the language. It is also a good introduction to the language and programming techniques using Prolog. Another good text is Clark and McCabe (1984), although this one is based around an alternative implementation of the language that uses a different syntax from that of Clocksin and Mellish.

Clark and Tarnlund (1982) is a useful collection of papers on applications of Prolog. Kluzniak and Szpacowicz (1984) describes the language from the point of view of someone who is already well versed in programming. It considers the design of Prolog programs and their efficiency as well as a listing of a Prolog interpreter in Pascal. For a more formal view of the philosophy of logic programming, the reader could consult Hogger (1984), Kowalski (1979) and Robinson (1965). The implementation of Prolog is addressed by contributed chapters in Campbell (1984), whilst Bratko (1986) is a new textbook on the language that describes its use in artificial intelligence.

CHAPTER 3

The introductory chapter of Charniak and McDermott (1985) specifies the desiderata and basic principles of knowledge representation. Other sources describe the individual approaches in detail: Brachman (1979, 1983), Hendrix (1978), and Deliyanni and Kowalski (1979) describe semantic networks, whilst Duda *et al* (1978), describe their use in an expert system. An early language for frames is described in Roberts and Goldstein (1977) and Winston and Horn (1981). Fikes and Kehler (1985) is a more up-to-date discussion, based around KEE, a knowledge representation package for AI workstations. This is one article in the September 1985 Special Section of CACM on Knowledge Representation. Other papers in this issue are Hayes-Roth (1985) and Genesareth and Ginsberg (1985), which review rule-based systems and logic programming respectively.

Aikins (1983) describes the use of frames and production rules together in implementing an expert system.

CHAPTER 4

The references here are a little thin, as no general principles for development of IKBS applications are yet accepted by the research community. Both Hayes-Roth *et al.* (1983) and Addis (1985) offer alternative prescriptions. Davis and Lenat (1982) describes a system that was able to help the expert debug and extend a knowledge base interactively without the intervention of a human knowledge engineer. Bennett (1985) and Swartout (1983) describe interactive tools to help design and build a new knowledge base.

CHAPTER 5

To follow up on planning systems, Daniel (1984) reviews two systems from the literature, STRIPS and NOAH. STRIPS can be read about separately in

Fikes and Nilsson (1971). Details of the implementation of a planner in Prolog can be found in Kluzniak and Szpacowicz (1984).

Michalski, Carbonell and Mitchell (1983) is an excellent collection of chapters on several distinct approaches to machine learning. Bundy (1984a) questions whether machine learning techniques are yet applicable to expert systems.

The application of AI techniques to computer-aided learning is also a field that is still only documented in research papers and volumes of conference or workshop proceedings. Volume II of Barr and Feigenbaum (1982) contains excellent summaries of some of the early work, and Sleeman and Brown (1984) is a collection of papers describing more recent work on intelligent tutoring systems.

CHAPTER 6

For general background on both the description of languages and computer processing of natural language, Winograd (1983) is an excellent introduction. For the reader who is interested in competing linguistic theories and formalisms, and in different approaches to parsing, King (1984) is a useful follow-up collection of tutorial papers. The Prolog Definite Clause Grammar (DCG) approach was first described in Pereira and Warren (1979), and further applications of this approach are among the references to Chapter 8. Dahl and Saint-Dizier (1985) is a collection of papers on DCG natural language processing. Some of these papers relate the DCG approach to current linguistic theories. Thompson and Ritchie (1984) show in detail how parsers based on two distinct approaches can be implemented in Lisp.

CHAPTER 7

Relative to syntax, semantics of natural language is a relatively underdeveloped field, and I cannot recommend a suitable text. Mellish (1985) shows how semantics was handled in understanding mechanics problems, and McCord (1982) and Warren and Pereira (1982) do the same for databases. All of these use logical notations which are easily applied in their restricted problem domains, but do not generalize to a theory of meaning for natural languages.

Schank's theory of conceptual understanding, based on a psychological viewpoint, is well presented in Schank and Abelson (1977) and in Schank (1982). Practical implementation of language understanding programs under this paradigm is discussed in Schank and Riesbeck (1981) and Dyer (1983).

CHAPTER 8

The general idea of a knowledge-based front end to existing unfriendly software is described by Bundy (1984), and further references are given there. There is current work in this area under the Alvey and ESPRIT programmes, and the proceedings of the ESPRIT Technical Week to be held in September 1986 should contain progress reports.

Hendrix *et al.* (1978) describes an early natural language database interface, whilst Konologe (1979) and Boguraev and Sparck-Jones (1982) both discuss a more rational architecture for such applications. Dahl (1982), McCord (1982) and Warren and Pereira (1982) all discuss database interfaces constructed within the DCG framework. Application of natural language understanding to operating systems is described in Wilensky (1984) and Hayes and Carbonell (1983).

BIBLIOGRAPHY

Addis, T. R. (1985). *Designing Knowledge-Based Systems*, Kogan Page, London. The book consists of two main parts: an exposition of techniques of conceptual data modelling and database design, and an introduction to artificial intelligence techniques. The author argues, with the support of worked examples, that the former are needed in designing applied systems that employ AI techniques.

Aikins, J. S. (1983). Prototypical knowledge for expert systems. *Artificial Intelligence* **20**, 163–210. Presents an approach to representing knowledge in expert consulting systems that is based on the idea of 'prototypes' of situations. The consultation is seen as an attempt to match prototypes onto the facts of the present case. The discussion is based on the CENTAUR system which integrates frames representing prototypical clinical entities and production rules in a re-implementation of the PUFF system for the management of obstructive airways disease.

Alty, J. L. and Coombs, M. J. (1984). *Expert Systems: Concepts and Examples*, NCC, Manchester. An introductory text on expert systems, which contains descriptions of eight systems from the research literature.

Barr, A. and Feigenbaum, E. A. (1982). *Handbook on Artificial Intelligence Vols I and II*, Pitman. These are part of a three-volume collection of articles on many of the programs developed in most sub-fields of artificial intelligence. These two volumes include sections on expert systems, natural language interfaces, intelligent computer-aided instruction and tutoring, as well as fields within AI (such as vision) that have not been treated in the present volume.

Bennett, J. S. (1985). ROGET: A knowledge-based system for acquiring the conceptual structure of a diagnostic expert system. *Journal of Automated Reasoning* **1**, 49–74. The ROGET system is an interactive knowledge-engineering tool designed to help with the initial stage of determining the conceptual structure of the system. It does this by reference to a knowledge base which describes abstractly the conceptual structure of the generic class of consultation programs and a number of subclasses and specific instances.

Boguraev, B. K. and Sparck-Jones, K. (1982). A natural language analyser for database access. *Information Technology: Research and Development* **1**, 23–39. An approach to the construction of natural language database interfaces is described which makes as much use as possible of domain independent syntactic and semantic knowledge, so as to make systems as portable as possible. The system uses an ATN parser and procedures for semantic analysis based on Wilks' preference semantics.

Brachman, R. J. (1979). On the epistemological status of semantic networks. *Associative networks: Representation and Use of Knowledge by Computers, N. V. Findler (ed)*, pp. 3–50, Academic Press, New York. The early part of this paper is particularly useful for its survey of the history of semantic networks. The subsequent discussion of the different meanings attached to the arcs in networks by different authors is instructive.

Brachman, R. J. (1983). What IS-A is and isn't: An analysis of taxonomic links in semantic networks. *COMPUTER* 30–36. A brief statement of the main arguments in Brachman (1979).

Bratko, I. (1986). *Prolog Programming for Artificial Intelligence.* Addison-Wesley, Wokingham. This book is divided into two sections: an introduction to the language, and a comprehensive and thorough review of its application in artificial intelligence. Most of the latter half of the book examines the detailed implementation of general problem solving and search methods in Prolog, but there is a chapter on building an expert system shell in Prolog.

Bundy, A. (1984). *What has Learning got to do with Expert Systems?* Department of Artificial Intelligence Research Paper No. 214, University of Edinburgh. Presents a review of the relevance of work on machine learning to the knowledge acquisition problem in expert systems. Concludes that inductive learning is only successful in systems that are so small or straightforward that the knowledge acquisition problem is trivial.

Bundy, A. (1984). *Intelligent Front Ends.* Edinburgh University, Department of Artificial Intelligence, Research Paper No. 227, Edinburgh. (Also in Pergamon Infotech State of the Art Report: Expert Systems, Pergamon.) This report reviews existing work on intelligent front ends and considers the software requirements, concluding that, in principle, a class of general-purpose packages like expert system shells, but specifically designed for IFEs, can be specified. A number of techniques for the various sub-tasks that an IFE must take on are described, including dialogue control, translation, synthesis and inference.

Campbell, J. A. (ed.) (1984). *Implementations of Prolog.* Ellis Horwood, Chichester. A collection of contributed articles on various aspects of the operation of a Prolog interpreter and its implementation. Also included are chapters on other languages using similar constructs, and the provision of Prolog-style theorem proving in Lisp.

Cendrowska, J. and Bramer, M. A. (1984). A rational reconstruction of the MYCIN consultation system. *International Journal of Man-Machine Studies.* Special edition on Developments in Expert Systems Part 3. Comprises a discussion of the authors' reconstruction of MYCIN in POP11 and a complete listing of the program and partial knowledge base. The description of the internal knowledge representation and operation of the system is clear, and the listings are useful as a rare published source of a realistic knowledge base. The article, minus the listings, is also reprinted as Chapter 15 of O'Shea and Eisenstadt (1984).

Charniak, E. and McDermott, D. (1985). *Introduction to Artificial Intelligence,* Addison-Wesley, Reading, Mass. A good text on AI emphasizing the more up to date approaches based on knowledge-based methods and using Lisp throughout in detailed examples. Has more emphasis on recognizable applications, including vision, language parsing and understanding, expert systems, planning and learning. Very readable, but without sacrificing rigour.

Clancey, W. J. (1983). The epistemology of a rule-based system. A framework for explanation. *Artificial Intelligence* 20, 215–251. Based on the author's research into the construction of a system for teaching medical diagnosis and treatment, the paper critically examines the weaknesses of a mechanical approach to justification in expert systems, and describes the approach taken in the NEOMYCIN system to incorporate a richer representation of domain knowledge in the system to augment the production rule knowledge-base.

Clark, K. L. and Tarnlund, S.-A. (eds) (1982). *Logic Programming (APIC Studies in Data Processing Vol 16)*. Academic Press, London. A conference proceedings with papers illustrating applications of Prolog as well as its theory and implementation.

Clark, K. L. and McCabe, F. G. (1984). *Micro-PROLOG: Programming in Logic*. Prentice-Hall, Englewood Cliffs, New Jersey. An introduction to Prolog based on an implementation developed at Imperial College, London. This implementation described is different in syntax from that described in Clocksin and Mellish's text, but is widely available for micro and minicomputers. The book concludes with extended case studies of the applications of Prolog including expert systems and operational research.

Clocksin, W. F. and Mellish, C. S. (1984). *Programming in Prolog* 2nd edn. Springer-Verlag, Berlin. The first and still probably the best textbook on Prolog. Widely used to define a standard version of the language. Discusses the language from several points of view: Prolog as a practical programming language, the operation of the interpreter, the relationship of Prolog to logic, list processing, applications with natural language and with graphs.

Coelho, H., Cotta, J. C. and Pereira, L. M. (1982). *How to Solve it with Prolog*. Laboratorio Nacional de Engenharia Civil, Lisbon (available from Expert Systems International, Oxford). A collection of example programs in Prolog. Several application areas are illustrated, but comments on the programs are sparse.

Coombs, M. J. (1984). *Developments in Expert Systems*. Academic Press, London. A collection of papers selected from the three-part special issue of the *International Journal of Man–Machine Studies* in 1984.

Danl, V. (1982). On database systems development through logic. *ACM Transactions on Database Systems* 7 (1), 102–123. This paper describes an integrated relational database system and natural language query processor, all developed uniformly in Prolog.

Dahl, V. and Saint-Dizier, P. (1985). *Natural Language Understanding and Logic Programming*. North-Holland, Amsterdam. A collection of papers presented at the First International Workshop on Natural Language Understanding and Logic Programming held in Rennes, France in 1984. The papers address a wide variety of technical and more theoretical issues. Particularly interesting are those that show how current linguistic theories can be realized within the DCG framework.

Daniel, L. (1984), in O'Shea and Eisenstadt (1984). A chapter on planning systems, which contains detailed reviews of STRIPS and NOAH.

Davis, R. and Lenat, D. B. (1982). *Knowledge-Based Systems in Artificial Intelligence*. McGraw Hill, New York. Half of this book is devoted to a discussion of Teiresias, Davis' program for knowledge-base refinement through a direct dialogue between expert and machine.

Deliyanni, A. and Kowalski, R. A. (1979). Logic and semantic networks. *Communications of the ACM* 22 (3), 184–192. Discusses an extended semantic network notation and its equivalence to clausal logic.

Duda, R. O., Hart, P. E., Nilsson, N. J. and Sutherland, G. L. (1978). Semantic network representations in rule-based inference systems. *Pattern Directed Inference Systems*, edited by D. A. Waterman and F. Hayes-Roth. Academic Press, New York. Describes the use of semantic networks in the PROSPECTOR expert system.

Dyer, M. E. (1983). *In-Depth Understanding*. MIT Press, Cambridge, Mass. Based on a PhD thesis. The author has developed a program which implements many of the theoretical notions of Schank (1982). A listing of a didactic micro-version is given as an appendix.

Fikes, R. and Kehler, T. (1985). The role of frame-based representation in reasoning.

Communications of the ACM **28** (9), 904–920. This paper begins with a review of the general characteristics of frame-based representation systems, including structural features and related inference mechanisms. It then goes on to discuss the use of a frame system in support of rule-based expert systems. The illustrative examples in the paper are encoded in the notation of KEE (Knowledge Engineering Environment), one of a small number of software products available on AI workstations.

Fikes, R. E. and Nilsson, N. J. (1971). STRIPS: A new approach to the application of theorem proving to problem solving. *Artificial Intelligence* **2**, 189–208. The original published description on STRIPS, the Stanford Research Institute Problem Solver.

Genesareth, M. R. and Ginsberg, M. L. (1985). Logic programming. *Communications of the ACM* **28** (9), 933–941. A tutorial discussion of logic programming within a special section on knowledge representation. The modelling of a logic circuit is used as a case study.

Gray, P. M. D. (1984). *Logic, Algebra and Databases*. Wiley, Chichester. Not primarily about Prolog, but shows its relationship to databases and, in particular, relational calculus query languages, such as Query-by-Example.

Haack, S. (1980). Do we need fuzzy logic? *International Journal of Man–Machine Studies*. Presents a critique of Zadeh's proposals for a fuzzy logic, especially of the concept of 'linguistic truth values'.

Hayes, P. J. and Carbonell, J. G. (1983). *A Framework for Processing Corrections in Task-Oriented Dialogues*, pp. 668–670. Proceedings of the Eighth International Joint Conference on Artificial Intelligence, Karlsruhe, W. Germany, 8–12 August 1983. This paper discusses the analysis of the meaning of meta-linguistic utterances (utterances about other utterances) in the context of an operating system where the user wishes to undo or modify the effect of requests made in error.

Hayes-Roth, F., Waterman, D. A. and Lenat, D. B. (1983). *Building Expert Systems*. Addison Wesley, Reading, Mass. A wide-ranging synthesis of the experience of 38 researchers into expert systems, discussing the architecture and development of expert systems, knowledge and reasoning, tools, languages and evaluation. A case study is presented in which several teams developed a prototype system for a single problem, each using different software tools. The diversity of the solutions illustrates the extent to which systems are more constrained by features of the implementing software rather than analysis of the problem. Although much of the general discussion of methods is available elsewhere, the book is a valuable source of reference for its detailed reviews of a range of specific software tools and languages. (However, the latter do not include the many recent inexpensive shells available in the UK.)

Hayes-Roth, F. (1985). Rule-based systems. *Communications of the ACM* **28** (9), 921–932. A tutorial discussion of production systems and their application in expert problem-solving systems.

Hendrix, G. G. (1978). *Encoding Knowledge in Partitioned Networks*. Technical Note 164, SRI International, Menlo Park, California. This technical report expounds in detail the use of partitioned networks to represent knowledge in a way that corresponds directly to predicate logic notation. In particular, it shows how to represent explicitly disjunction, negation and existential quantification, which is not possible in other logic-based notation. Briefer descriptions of the partitioned network formalism by Hendrix are to be found in the 1975 and 1977 IJCAI conference proceedings and in the collection by Findler (see Brachman, 1979).

Hendrix, G. G., Sacerdoti, E. D., Sagalowicz, D. and Slocum, J. (1978). Developing a natural language interface to complex data. *ACM Transactions on Database Systems* **3** (2), 105–147. This paper describes a project called 'Ladder' (Language Access to Distributed Databases with Error Recovery) which incorporated the LIFER natural language dialogue system. The distinguishing features of LIFER are the processing of incomplete (elliptical) inputs and run-time user enhancement of the system's knowledge of words and syntactic rules.

Hogger, C. J., *Introduction to Logic Programming*. Academic Press, London. An advanced text on the logical foundations of Prolog, the principles of logic programming, program verification, implementation of the interpreter and its data structures, and a consideration of the impact of Prolog on the wider world of computer science.

Jacobs, P. S. (1985). PHRED: A generator for natural language interfaces. *Computational Linguistics* 11 (4), 219–242. Describes the operation and linguistic knowledge-base of PHRED, the language generation component of the UC system (see Wilensky, 1984).

Kidd, A. (1985). MMI issues in the construction and use of an expert system. *International Journal of Man-Machine Studies* 22, 91–102. Discusses representation and human factors issues arising from experience in constructing an expert system for electronic fault-finding using an expert system shell. Raises the issue of meta-knowledge concerning the actual inference strategies used by expert problem solvers which differed from the backward chaining mechanism provided by the shell.

King, M. (1984). *Parsing Natural Language*. Academic Press, London. A collection of articles on different issues and methods of parsing. Based on a tutorial workshop rather than a conference.

Kluzniak, F. and Szpakowicz, S. (1984). *Prolog for Programmers*. Academic Press, London. Gives an advanced treatment of the language, and discusses program design and efficiency, as well as explaining the background to Prolog in resolution and unification. Presents a case study of Prolog for a sophisticated application (WARPLAN, a planning system developed by David Warren) and a complete Prolog interpreter written in Pascal.

Konolige, K. (1979). *A Framework for a Portable Natural-Language Interface to Large Databases*. Technical Note 197, SRI International, 333 Ravenswood Ave., Menlo Park, California 94025. Based on experience with the Ladder system (see Hendrix, 1978), this work is concerned to establish an architecture for portable natural language database interfaces, using conceptual database schemas to hide the data description and query languages of individual database systems from the front end language processor.

Kowalski, R. A. (1979). *Logic for Problem Solving*. Elsevier-North Holland, New York. A presentation of the arguments for logic programming as an alternative computing paradigm.

McCord, M. C. (1982). Using slots and modifiers in logic grammars for natural language. *Artificial Intelligence* 18, 327–367. A linguistic formalism: for each syntactic structure a central predication, a cluster of modifiers, a set of features and a determiner is outlined, together with its implementation in Prolog using the Definite Clause Grammar notation. This form of grammar encompasses much information besides phrase structure which is relevant to semantic interpretation. The associated semantic interpretation routines are capable of a sophisticated analysis of quantifiers. The usefulness of the approach is demonstrated by the construction of a database query interface. The paper is accompanied by listings of all the important parts of the language analyser together with samples of input and output.

Mellish, C. (1985). *Computer Interpretation of Natural Language Descriptions*. Ellis Horwood Series in Artificial Intelligence, Chichester. Unlike most natural language interfaces, the system described here has been concerned with the semantic analysis of descriptive text rather than questions. The context in which the work was done was a system called 'MECHO' which solved school mechanics problems expressed in English. These problems were concerned with rods, strings and pulleys, but often the numbers of these objects and their relationships to other objects could not be established by semantic analysis within the confines of a single sentence. The approach described here is to build up a semantic analysis as a set of Prolog assertions incrementally.

Michalksi, R. S. and Chilauski, R. L. (1980). Learning by being told and learning from examples: An experimental comparison of the two methods of knowledge acquisition in the context of developing an expert system for soybean disease diagnosis. *Policy Analysis and Information Systems* **4**. The title is so long that no further description is needed!

Michalski, R. S., Carbonell, J. G. and Mitchell, T. M. (1983). *Machine Learning*, Tioga Palo Alto, CA. A significant collection of contributed papers describing the state of the art in various approaches to machine learning. Carbonell, Michalski and Mitchell's overview chapter presents a useful classification of styles of learning. Dietterich and Michalski's chapter reviews machine learning programs. Haas and Hendrix's chapter describes Nanoklaus, a system for knowledge acquisition from natural language dialogue. Carbonell's chapter describes work on intelligent tutoring systems.

O'Shea, T. and Eisenstadt, M. (1984). *Artificial Intelligence, Tools, Techniques and Applications*. Harper & Row, New York. A textbook that has been assembled from separately contributed chapters presented at a summer school on AI. Divided into three sections (as indicated by the sub-title). The first section reviews Prolog, Lisp (most emphasis), and POP11 as tools for AI. The techniques section contains two chapters on basic techniques in robotics and one on natural language parsing. Applications covered include vision, natural language processing, industrial robotics, text processing, planning and OR, and expert systems. Some of the individual contributions are good, but coverage of the field is uneven.

Pereiera, F. C. N. and Warren. D. H. D. (1980). Definite clause grammars for natural language analysis – A survey of the formalism and comparison with augmented transition networks. *Artificial Intelligence* **13**, 231–278. A clear and powerful formalism for describing languages follows from a method for expressing grammars in logic due to Colmerauer and Kowalski. The formalism is a natural extension of context free grammars. A DCG not only describes a language – it is, as it stands, an executable Prolog program. The DCG has the same power as an ATN, and in practice is more concise and efficient.

Roberts, R. B. and Goldstein, I. P. (1977). *The FRL Primer*, Report AIM–408, Massachusetts Institute of Technology, Cambridge, Mass. Provides an introduction and abridged manual to the FRL frame representation language.

Robinson, J. A. (1965). A machine-oriented logic based on the resolution principle. *Journal of the ACM* **12**, 23–41. The original paper describing the principle of resolution theorem proving.

Schank, R. C. and Abelson, R. P. (1977). *Scripts, Plans, Goals and Understanding*. Lawrence Erlbaum, Hillsdale, NJ. Outlines a programme of research on the memory structures needed to account for the inferences made in comprehending natural language texts.

Schank, R. C. and Riesbeck, C. K. (1981). *Inside Computer Understanding: Five programs plus miniatures*. Lawrence Erlbaum, Hillsdale, NJ. A tutorial text describing the underlying principles of the Yale natural language understanding programs and their implementation. Microversions of the programs are described in detail.

Schank, R. C. (1982). *Dynamic Memory*. Cambridge University Press, New York. An update on Schank and Abelson (1977) focusing on dynamic processes of reminding and learning rather than on static memory structures like scripts.

Shortliffe, E. H. (1976). *Computer-Based Medical Consultations: MYCIN*. North Holland, Amsterdam. Derived from the author's PhD thesis, this book gives a general overview of the MYCIN expert system and its construction.

Sleeman, D. H. and Brown, J. S. (1984). *Intelligent Tutoring Systems.* Academic Press, London. A collection of papers documenting recent work on intelligent tutoring systems.

Swartout, W. R. (1983). XPLAIN: A system for creating and explaining expert consulting programs. *Artificial Intelligence,* **21,** 285–325. The program described here is concerned with improving the explanation of the behaviour of expert consulting programs. It does this by using a domain model consisting of descriptive facts and domain principles to generate an expert system. The system has been applied to the reconstruction of a Digitalis Therapy Advisor.

Thompson, H. and Ritchie, G. (1984). Implementing natural language parsers. In O'Shea and Eisenstadt, *Artificial Intelligence: Tools, Techniques and Applications,* pp. 245–300. Harper & Row, London.

Winston, P.H. and Horn, B. K. P. (1981). *LISP.* Addison-Wesley, Reading, Mass. Chapter 22 describes the FRL language of Roberts and Goldstein (1977) and shows how frames and their associated procedures can be implemented in LISP.

Winston, P. H. (1984). *Artificial Intelligence* 2nd ed. Addison-Wesley, Reading, Mass. A well-respected text on basic AI techniques. Complemented by Winston and Horn's LISP text.

INDEX